THE ECONOMICS OF DISTRIBUTION

The Economics of Distribution

Manager's guide to trade-off
and cost control in physical distribution

L C W SAWDY

A Halsted Press Book

John Wiley & Sons
New York

First published in Britain by Gower Press Limited
Epping, Essex
1972

Published in the USA
by Halsted Press, a Division of
John Wiley & Sons, Inc.
New York.

ISBN 0 470 75548 2

Library of Congress Catalog Card No. 72–7833

Set in 11 on 13 Times and printed by
A. Wheaton & Co., Great Britain

Contents

Illustrations

Introduction

"*People who like this sort of thing will find this the sort of thing they like*"
ABRAHAM LINCOLN

There is little doubt that, during the nineteen-seventies, the distribution function will be getting the detailed cost scrutiny that has hitherto been reserved for manufacturing and selling. Varied estimates have been put forward as to what the percentage cost of distribution is, but they have to be treated with reserve, because many firms have little idea of what distribution really costs and the percentage can vary widely according to the type of business and the costs it is considered relevant to include under the heading of distribution.

Most authorities are agreed, however, that this is the one area of cost saving that has not been fully explored. Moreover, it is no good leaving specialist distribution men to explore it alone because distribution encroaches on manufacture and selling to a degree that is very little appreciated. It is the one function where trade-off economics come into play, that is to say, where a deliberate increase in the unit cost of one activity can result in a correspondingly greater saving in the unit cost of another.

There are two aspects to distribution. One, under the general heading of industrial engineering, is concerned more with the practical application of distribution—the running of warehouses and transport fleets, the selection and use of materials-handling equipment, packaging, documentation and so on. Considerable knowledge and study has been brought to bear on these subjects and much valuable work has been written on them.

The other side of the coin is concerned with the economics of distribution and with the effect that one activity can have on another in the process of delivering goods to customers in the most economic manner. Here it is true to say that the state of knowledge is still fairly limited and considerable scope exists for further study and research.

This book is concerned purely with the economic aspects of distribution and is believed to bring together, for the first time, all those strands of inter-related knowledge that are woven into the fabric of distribution economics. It is not written in technical language because it is designed to communicate the principles of the subject to a wide audience—to production people, to sales people, to financial people and most of all to general management, because it is these who must be able to view the whole economic jig-saw and see what pieces fit where.

The wide-ranging incidence of distribution economics is perhaps one reason for its past neglect. It involves too many people who might prefer to remain aloof from it. It suggests the need for new attitudes of mind and new approaches to corporate organisation.

But markets are becoming larger and more diffuse and manufacturing units are becoming fewer. The widening of international trade horizons is increasing the distance between the consumer and the production unit.

In these changing circumstances, it is reasonable to suggest that industrial performance will depend more and more on establishing a harmonious economic relationship between manufacture, delivery and sale and it is not too great an exaggeration to say that this is as good a definition of distribution as any.

The real economics of distribution are trade-off economies, namely, finding the best combination of two or more costs so that the total is minimised even though one of the components actually goes up.

The principal areas of trade-off economies can be summarised as follows:

Purchasing versus stock

1 Is the value of buying discounts greater than the cost of holding the incurred stock?

Manufacturing versus stock

2 Is it cheaper to manufacture at the most economic level and store the surplus in periods of low demand, or would it pay to vary production according to demand even at a higher unit cost?

Lead time versus stock or sales volume

3 Is the cost of reducing lead time (by using faster transport, for example, or by streamlining order processing) more than outweighed either by inventory savings or by increased sales?

Sales versus stock

4 Is it cheaper to lose a sale than to gain it by holding stock?

There are, of course, many variations on these four themes. Is it cheaper to store at the point of manufacture, at the point of sale or some intermediate point? What happens when different autonomous companies are involved in the same process of distribution? What differences exist between national distribution and international distribution?

But the principles are always the same. Grasp the principles and they apply to any process of manufacturing and selling products.

There are three chapters in this book that might at first sight appear to be out of place in a work on distribution economics or, at any rate, to lay undue emphasis on the matters they discuss.

Distribution cost accounting is dealt with in Chapter 1. The biggest single barrier to improved distribution efficiency is lack of information on individual costs. Unless one knows what the costs are now, it is impossible to determine whether or not they can be reduced. The importance of adequate accounting cannot be over-emphasised.

Sales forecasting is described in Chapter 2. This is not a lesson on the methods of forecasting but a plea not to expect more from forecasts than they can give. The costs of distribution are very largely based on what is expected to be sold. If all the eggs of distribution are put into the one basket of a narrow sales forecast, there is a frightening probability that all the eggs will be smashed. The error inherent in forecasting must be accepted and acted upon.

Chapter 10 is concerned with demands on the organisation. The special importance of organisation to distribution lies in the existence of trade-off economies. Unless conventional organisation is modified to take account of the fact that a variety of functions are directly involved in the distribution function, there will be natural but fatal human resistance to change. Without the right organisation, distribution can become an academic ideal—everyone agrees with it so long as it only applies to someone else's street.

Finally let management beware of acceding to proposals they do not understand. In discussing "high finance or the point of vanishing interest", Professor Parkinson once argued that if a proposal is so complex and costly that the executives responsible for appraising it do not fully comprehend it, it is far more likely to receive approval than if the subject matter is something they all know about. There are many areas of distribution that can be susceptible to fairly sophisticated mathematical treatment—inventory control, depot location and so on—and management will often fail to understand the specialised techniques that are used. The danger is the familiar one of the specialist over-estimating the significance of his speciality.

The principles of distribution economics are not difficult to understand and any executive who does understand them will soon be able to hack through the jungle of algebraic formulae to make sure he is building a distribution operation on firm ground.

1

Accounting for the cost of distribution

"It is a capital mistake to theorise before one has data"
SIR ARTHUR CONAN DOYLE

Many discussions about reducing distribution costs come to an abrupt close because the participants find that they do not know what their distribution costs are at present. There is no point in considering change if there is no knowledge of what it is that is to be changed.

Conventional Accounting Does Not Isolate Distribution Costs

There are two reasons for the lack of information. One is that conventional accounting systems do not isolate the costs of distribution, which tend to be put into a general expenses category.

The simplied version of a conventional accounts presentation given in Figure 1:1 focuses on the three traditional areas of expense—direct labour, material and sales cost. Transport, warehousing, packing and other distribution costs are not given as separate headings. They may be found in works overhead, general expenses or some other category. Auditors are not interested in distribution as a separate accounts classification.

The second reason is that, even if distribution costs are classified separately, they often do not provide information of economic significance.

For example, a company might keep very detailed records of the cost of running its transport fleet—depreciation, running costs, maintenance, labour and so on. They can compare the costs of one year with those of a previous year; they can express transport costs as a percentage of sales turnover or total cost and compare the percentages from one year to another but such data, studied in isolation, can be misleading. For, what is significant, from an economic standpoint, is not the cost of transport, but the cost of delivery, which is an entirely different matter. A study of Figure 1:2 shows that an analysis of the transport cost per mile would, in this example, be entirely misleading. If improved routing, or larger average drop size, resulted in a lower total mileage for the same volume of delivery,

Gross sales	£550 000	
Freight, royalties, commissions	£16 500	
Net sales	£533 500	
Material purchases	£108 000	
Direct labour	£152 000	£260 000
Gross profit		£273 500
Indirect labour	£85 000	
Selling expenses	£60 000	
General expenses	£73 000	£218 000
		£55 000

FIGURE 1:1 ACCOUNTS PRESENTATION

Total mileage	Transport cost per mile (pence)	Total transport costs (£)	Sales (£)	Transport costs as percentage of sales
30 000	11	3 375	50 000	6.75
25 000	12½	3 125	50 000	6.25

FIGURE 1:2 TRANSPORT COSTS

	Pence
Vehicle trunking cost per mile	20
Delivery van cost per mile	6
AREA A	
100 trunking miles @ 20p	2000
600 delivery miles @ 6p	3600
	5600
Number of drops = 40	
Average delivery per drop — 10 units	
Average delivery cost per unit =	14
Average delivery cost per drop =	140
AREA B	
200 trunking miles @ 20p	4000
200 delivery miles @ 6p	1200
	5200
Number of drops = 10	
Average delivery per drop — 40 units	
Average delivery cost per unit = $\frac{5200}{400}$ =	13
Average delivery cost per drop = $\frac{5200}{10}$ =	520

FIGURE 1:3 DISTRIBUTION OF CAKES

the transport cost per mile would go up, but the transport cost per unit delivered would drop, and this is the important criterion. Figure 1:3 compares the cost of transporting cakes to two different areas and shows that, although area B is twice as far away as area A, the delivery cost per unit is lower, because the drop size is larger, and perhaps also the routing more efficient.

Further analysis might reveal even more scope for economy. In area A, for example, *the average* delivery cost per unit is fourteen pence, but if the drop size is analysed in further detail, as in Figure 1:4, it soon becomes evident that ten of the drops are so small that they are uneconomic. Either a premium delivery charge must be levied or the business rejected because the additional delivery costs are reducing the profit.

Number of drops = 40
Average delivery per drop = 10 units

Number of drops	Units per drop	Delivery cost per unit (pence)
10	4	35
10	10	14
10	11	12·7
10	15	9·3

FIGURE 1:4 DROP SIZE

Transport Costs

Adequate cost data are required to determine the type of vehicle it is most economic to use in any business.

Figure 1:5 compares the cost of running four different types of truck for 36 000 miles a year.

	Vehicle type			
	8-ton Rigid	16-ton Rigid	16-ton Artic	22-ton Artic
Fixed Costs (£)				
Licences	185	350	400	520
Insurance	150	200	250	300
Depreciation	400	520	500	600
Sub-total	735	1070	1150	1420
Semi-variable costs (£)				
Wages	1600	1600	1600	1600
Maintenance	1025	1270	1380	1550
Sub-total	2625	2870	2980	3150
Variable costs (£)				
Petrol and oil	820	1250	1250	1400
TOTAL PER ANNUM	4180	5190	5380	5970

FIGURE 1:5 RUNNING COSTS RELATED TO VEHICLE SIZE

The only completely fixed costs are licences and insurance. If any vehicle were to increase its mileage beyond 36 000 miles, the wage bill would go up and the depreciation cost would be greater. But these costs by themselves are not truly significant. Since a vehicle is only in economic use when it is moving with a revenue-paying load, what is needed is information about how much time is spent in the garage, on maintenance, loading and unloading, whether, or not, the vehicle is fully loaded for each trip, the size of each drop in relation to its value, the mileage for each drop, and so on.

A more sophisticated approach to the problem of costing transport in delivery might take account of the relationship between the route mileage and the decreasing payload of the vehicle after each drop was made. If a truck starts off full and makes ten drops before it is emptied, then the cost of each subsequent drop increases because the running costs of the vehicle have to be borne by a diminishing payload. This would hold completely true on the assumption that, in reaching the final delivery point, the vehicle did not have to depart from the most direct route in order to make the intermediate drops. If the vehicle did have to depart from the most direct route, allowance would have to be made for this factor in costing each drop. A detailed example of the factors involved is given in Chapter 3, Figure 3:13. The principle to bear in mind is that the true cost per drop of a five-drop journey is not the total cost of the journey divided by five. It may very well prove to be impracticable to attempt to maintain cost records in this sort of detail but the realisation of these economics could very well result in an awareness that it might, for example, be cheaper to give some of the more distant drops to a public carrier than to attempt to do them oneself.

Warehousing Costs

It is not difficult to determine the cost of running a warehouse. There is, first of all, depreciation or rental on the building and any equipment used inside it such as racking, conveyors and fork-lift trucks. Secondly, there is the cost of the personnel required for handling, documentation and management. Necessary services such as fuel, electricity and water have also to be taken into account. There might be taxes or other costs associated with a particular area. Whilst it is essential to maintain and scrutinise these expenses, these are not usually the major costs of keeping stock. The main costs are those associated with the product being stored—its value, and any deterioration that takes place in its value, during the period of storage. The cost associated with the product value is the cost of the money tied up in the product. It has to be borne in mind that this cost is not a standard figure common to all economic circumstances. One firm, for example, might have plenty of money available from which it is receiving seven per cent interest, so that the real cost of money tied up in stock is seven per cent. Another firm might be short of money and have to borrow at nine per cent to finance the stock; the cost to them is therefore nine per cent. Yet another business might be urgently seeking cash for an investment from which it expects to earn twenty-five per cent; the value of any money that can be saved in stock rises here to twenty-five per cent.

Deterioration in value while a product is in storage is generally due to two causes. The first is actual physical damage or deterioration. This means that customers will either not be willing to buy it at all or only at a reduced price, for example, a shop-soiled garment. The second is where the product becomes obsolescent during the period of storage with a consequent affect on its value. An example of obsolescence is where a garment goes out of fashion.

For all these reasons, the cost of storage expressed as a percentage of the product being stored can range between extremes of, say, five per cent and thirty per cent.

Although the principal determination of storage cost is how long the product stays in the warehouse, it does not necessarily follow that it is economic to reduce the period of storage, as described in Chapter 7. If this reduction results in lost sales, then the profit value of the lost sales must be compared to the additional storage cost necessary to avoid those lost sales.

The Cost Relationships of Stock

In subsequent chapters it will be shown that stock stands in economic relationship to three other business functions.

1 *Manufacturing cost (including buying)* The lowest unit cost of manufacture will usually involve availability of finished product in excess of demand during certain periods. The surplus creates a stock cost. If this stock is significant in size, it is possible that a lower volume of manufacture at a higher unit cost might be a more economic alternative, at certain periods, to a high stock level. To make this calculation, it is necessary to know how the unit cost of manufacture varies with changes of output.

2 *Demand* The main factor here is the frequency distribution of demand. If demand ranges from ten units a week to forty units a week, how many weeks in the year will demand equal ten, how many fifteen, twenty-five, forty and so on. The more infrequently demand in any week rises to a high peak above the average, the greater the amount of safety stock that must be carried to satisfy the infrequent demand—see Chapter 4. The question that has to be answered is:

> Would it be cheaper to keep a lower level of stock and accept a certain level of lost sales or, can total profit be increased by raising stock? The incremental profit ensuing from the latter might be greater than the incremental stock cost.

The problem here is that the frequency distribution of demand can only be deduced from historical sales data which may not always be relevant to what will happen in the future, and indeed, involves fairly sophisticated calculations when related to the amount of safety stock necessary to satisfy that demand. The smaller company will not be justified in attempting to make precise calculations along these lines, but it is important that management should understand, and take into account, the economic principles involved.

3 *Lead Times* To satisfy any given demand, stock levels will be determined by the supply lead time—the time it takes for an order for fresh supplies to be fulfilled. The shorter the lead time, the lower the stock level required. It is, therefore, necessary to know the scope that exists for reducing lead time and the cost of so doing. This will usually mean a faster and more expensive means of transport, but a reduction in the time taken to process an order and the time taken to place it will also shorten lead time.

It is not enough, therefore, just to know the cost of holding stock and it is quite wrong to adopt some arbitrary or pre-conceived notion of what the stock level ought to be. Even if it is not practical to make precise computations, some sensible allowance must be made for these factors. A comparison of the two costs given in Figure 1:6 speaks for itself. The annual demand for motor spare parts is the same as for the motor accessory. But the consequences of not having the spare part in stock are far more serious than for the accessory.

	Motor vehicle	
	spare part	accessory
Annual sales—value (£)	10 000	10 000
Annual sales—volume (units)	1 000	1 000
Average stock level (£)	5 000	1 000
Annual stock cost (£)	1 000	200
Profit loss of each stock-out (£)	30	2
Cost of 10% stock reduction (£)	1500 − 100 = 1400	20 − 20 = Nil

FIGURE 1:6 COST COMPARISON

It is assumed that a ten per cent reduction in stock will result in a failure to supply on fifty occasions with the spare part and on ten occasions with the accessory. It will be noted that, in the latter example, the £20 saving on stock is balanced by the profit loss (also £20).

Although transport and warehousing make up the two principal costs of distribution, there are a number of other expenses that also go towards the cost of delivery to the customer; and some of these affect each other.

Packing Costs

Packaging, when not used purely for merchandising, is designed to protect the goods from damage and theft. This can affect the cost of insurance—which is sometimes lower when protection of the goods carried is known to be better, as with a sealed container. It can also affect the cost of transport because, if this is based on the weight of the complete package then heavy packaging cost can increase transport cost considerably—particularly for air freight. On the other hand, if the packing is inadequate, then damage or theft could affect ability to supply and this will prejudice future sales—a cost that could not be covered by insurance.

Documentation Costs

The amount of documentation often depends on the method of transport and the formalities required in a country of destination. This is also a function of internal procedures regarding order placing and processing. It is often enlightening to isolate and scrutinise documentation costs.

Cost of Obtaining Costs

The problem of maintaining adequate information on the cost of distribution is affected by two considerations. One, which has already been mentioned, is the cost of obtaining information. It is quite possible for this cost to be higher that the savings that can be achieved as a consequence of having the information. Common sense must be used in deciding the scope and detail of information that is recorded and it should be borne in mind that an order of magnitude can often have just as much utility as a precise calculation. What is important is that those concerned with distribution should be aware of all the possibilities so that sound judgements can be made about the degree of detail that is necessary.

Responsibility for Evaluating Costs

The other consideration concerns the responsibility for deciding on the information to be kept and who is to do the actual recording. This involves questions of organisation that are discussed fully in Chapter 10. What can be said here is that an individual in a company—no matter what his terms of reference are—must be directly charged with responsibility for evaluating all the variables in the distribution equation. Much of the work will no doubt be carried out by the accounts department, and the chief financial executive would undoubtedly have some worthwhile opinion and expertise to contribute to this problem. But, unless one individual is made responsible for surveying the whole structure, the danger is that only absolute costs will be scrutinised and not the effect of one cost on another.

Selling Costs

Whilst selling may not, at first sight, appear to be a cost of distribution, it must be remembered that the cost of selling a product can be so high, in relation to the volume sold, as to make it an uneconomic proposition.

It is quite easy for this to happen when a salesman is handling a number of different lines. For one reason or another—personal interest, high commission prospects, and so on—a disproportionate amount of time is spent on a product where the volume of sales is low. If the sales cost attributable to this particular product is isolated, it may exceed the gross profit left after all other costs have been taken into account. For example, a machine manufacturing company may wrongly assume there is a good market for a particular machine, spend money on leaflets, films, advertising and other forms of sales promotion, exhort salesmen to push the model and then subsequently find out that the market does not really exist.

It is important, therefore, to look at sales costs not only from the standpoint of the various elements of expenditure such as advertising, exhibitions and so on, but also from the standpoint of allocating this expenditure to the various products being sold. People working within a firm, particularly technicians, can often adopt a predisposition or attachment to a particular product idea that does not stand up to an objective market examination.

Summary

To summarise, a manufacturer needs to know the total cost of delivery per unit of product sold. In other words, how much is spent, over and above the cost of manufacture, in getting the goods to the customer.

The total list of information that needs to be recorded for this purpose is as follows:

STORAGE
- Rent
- Utilities
- Equipment
- Labour
- Interest
- Deterioration
- Obsolescence
- Replenishment lead time

OWN TRANSPORT
- Tax
- Insurance
- Labour
- Depreciation
- Oil and petrol
- Maintenance
- Alternative transport costs

HIRED TRANSPORT
- Rates

LOADING, UNLOADING, HANDLING
- Time-idle transport
- Labour
- Equipment

DELIVERY DROPS
- Size of drop
- Transport cost

PACKING
- Purchase cost of material
- Labour
- Transport cost of packing
- Container economics

LOST SALES
- Stock-out
- Profit loss

PRODUCTION COSTS

FREQUENCY DISTRIBUTION OF DEMAND
- Safety stock

COST OF SALES
- Analysed by product

Recording this information is one requirement; drawing the right conclusions from it is another. The relationships that have to be examined can be expressed in the form of questions to which answers must be sought:

1 When does it pay to use own transport and when does it pay to use an outside contractor?

The variables that have to be considered are the cost of own transport, the cost of hired transport, the number and geographical distribution of deliveries and the amount of each delivery.

2 What is the relationship between the method of transport used and other direct costs such as packing, documentation, handling and insurance?

3 What is the optimum level of safety stock in demand inventory?

The two variables to be equated are the frequency distribution of demand and the cost of lost sales. At what point does it pay to run out of stock?

4 What is the optimum relationship between the cost of manufacture and the volume of production inventory?

The costs to be scrutinised are the varying unit costs of manufacture at various levels of output compared to the cost of holding stock.

5 What is the most economic way to hold demand stock? At the point of manufacture? At an intermediate storage depot? or both?

The cost of trunking transport and the cost of delivery transport has to be related to the cost of holding stock at various geographical locations.

6 Does an analysis of sales expense reveal that the cost of selling one or more particular products is uneconomic?

Applicable where a number of different lines are being sold and the total cost of sales has to be apportioned as accurately as possible among the different lines.

Distribution Control Information for Management

The following information should be recorded wherever possible and scrutinised by management at regular intervals.

Transport

	This month	Last month	Previous month
(a) Total operating costs (£)			
(b) Ton-mile costs (pence)			
(c) Operating costs per drop (£)			
(d) Delivery cost per unit (pence)			

FIGURE 1:7 OWN VEHICLE OPERATING COSTS

This information will indicate:

1 Deterioration in the efficiency of vehicle operation and maintenance, i.e. (a) and (b)
2 Efficiency of vehicle scheduling, i.e. (b) and (c)
3 Any significant increase in (d) should be followed by an analysis of delivery costs by delivery points to determine if any uneconomic deliveries are taking place.

	This month	Last month	Previous month
(a) Total hiring cost (£) (b) Ton-mile cost (pence) (c) Delivery cost per unit (pence)			

FIGURE 1:8 HIRED ROAD TRANSPORT OPERATING COSTS

Where applicable, these costs should be compared to own transport costs.

Cost of	This month	Last month	Previous month
Rail freight (total) Rail freight (ton-mile) Sea freight Freight forwarding Freight container hiring or depreciation			

FIGURE 1:9 FREIGHT COSTS

Cost of	This period	Last period
Starting stock in units or value Receipts Despatches Finishing stock in units or value		
Average stock balance in warehouse		
Warehouse operating costs Stock investment Stock deterioration Stock obsolescence		
Total stock		
Stock costs as a percentage of average stock value		

FIGURE 1:10 AVERAGE STOCK COSTS

2

The effect of sales forecasting on distribution

"Life is the art of drawing sufficient conclusions from insufficient premises"
SAMUEL BUTLER

There is no such thing as a wrong sales forecast, if it is based on an accurate evaluation of all known data. It may be more probable on the facts that next year's sales will be above £100 000 rather than below it; if next year's sales turn out to be £90 000 this does not mean to say that the forecast was wrong; it merely means that what was less likely to happen has in fact come to pass.

Sales forecasting is crucial to distribution economics because the cost of distribution so often depends on how much there is to distribute. The better one knows beforehand what has to be delivered to certain customers by actual means, the more efficient one can plan to make that delivery. Uncertainty about demand is the main reason for keeping stock, and the cost of stock is, in general, a very important item in the cost of distribution. The same uncertainty can result in emergency transport costs, surplus inventory, obsolescence, lost sales and many other indirect expenses.

If the level of demand is known and constant; for example, one knows beforehand that the demand is always going to be a regular 100 or 1000 units a week, it is not necessary to keep any stock in order to satisfy all demand. Manufacturing capacity can be precisely geared to meet the known demand and the costs of distribution comprise only the packing of the product, transport to the customer and the documentation costs associated with these operations. There might be some in-transit stock awaiting transportation, but that is all.

If the level of demand is known beforehand but this demand is irregular and one knows, for example, that the precise monthly demand over the next twelve months is going to be 64, 90, 30, 76, 29, 18, 40, 42, 59, 70, 30 and 35 units respectively, then the only additional problem created by the irregularity of demand is how to manufacture this quantity in the most economic manner. On a continuous production process, this would involve a regular monthly output with the minimum stock necessary to meet above-average monthly demands.

On a batch production process, the most economic batch size would be geared to the variable monthly demand and again this would involve the maintenance of some finished stock and work-in-progress. However, the sole purpose of the stock would be to permit the most economic form of manufacture.

If the level of demand is not precisely known beforehand—the situation in real life—one is faced with the problem of how to measure, and deal with, this uncertain situation. Limits can be placed around the area of uncertainty and it can be safely assumed that weekly or daily demand will not fall below a certain minimum or rise above a certain maximum. It can further be assumed that within these limits there is less likelihood of actual demand in any week being near either limit than there is of it being near the middle of the range. If demand averages fifty units a week but never falls below thirty units a week or rises above seventy, it is obviously valid to conclude that a demand of thirty-two or sixty-eight in any week is much less likely to arise than a demand of forty-eight or fifty-two. Unlikely to arise—yes. But it might. And herein lies the problem. Should stock be kept to cover the more unlikely levels of demand—or would it be cheaper to accept an out-of-stock position on the occasions when demand does reach this level? These are questions of probability that can not only be difficult to measure but equally difficult to define.

The Law of Probability

The problems involved in sales forecasting derive from the law of probability. Forecasting is concerned not with an occurrence that *will* take place but with an occurrence that *might* take place. What is the likelihood of the customer buying—and if so, how much will be bought? Measuring this likelihood or probability is the function of the forecast.

Perhaps the best way to appreciate the problem is to return to the theme that there can be no such thing as a wrong forecast. When the weather man gives a forecast on television each evening, certain assumptions are made based on known data. It is *known* there is a depression centred off Iceland; and it is *known* that this is filling in at a certain rate. From past experience certain *deductions* can be made about the speed the weather front travels, the velocity of the wind, the density of the cloud, the temperature and so on. This is then translated into a forecast expressed in everyday terms. To be truly scientific, however, the forecast should read something like this:

> "The day will be sunny with a little variable cloud on the assumption that the high pressure front south of England moves in a north-easterly direction at 30 miles an hour and develops in a manner normal to this type of front in these conditions. If it moves in a southerly direction there will be rain and the amount of rain will depend on certain temperature and pressure conditions that are unpredictable."

When it rains heavily the following day it is natural, but not scientific, to curse the weather expert for a wrong forecast. He may have been unskilful in interpreting the data. It may just as well be, however, that his assumptions have been invalidated due to reasons that did not have a high degree of probability at the time the forecast was made.

There could, however, be another way to express the forecast. He could come to the screen and tell us there was a ninety-five per cent probability of a fine sunny day, an eighty-five per cent probability of sunny periods with occasional showers, a forty-five per cent probability of its being cloudy with intermittent rain and a twenty per cent probability of it being cloudy with continuous rain. Such a forecast, provided it was based on an accurate evaluation of all known data, would be perfectly proper and *would in fact be accurate no matter how the weather turned out.* It is very important for any business executive to appreciate this point.

In sales forecasting, there are two basic approaches which are described below.

Historical Data

One has to assume that what has happened in the past will continue to happen in the future. Subject to certain modifications and assumptions this seems reasonable in the light of current knowledge. To take a simple example, it is assumed that a manufacturer of vests is selling only to Marks and Spencers and that sales over the previous five years have been as shown in Figure 2:1.

£ × 1000

Month	Year				
	1	2	3	4	5
Jan	22	12	25	27	28
Feb	22	12	25	27	28
Mar	20	12	23	28	30
Apr	20	32	22	28	30
May	20	26	20	37	30
Jun	21	23	20	36	34
Jul	23	23	42	35	35
Aug	25	27	30	32	35
Sep	30	32	35	35	37
Oct	35	36	35	34	37
Nov	33	35	32	32	35
Dec	26	30	30	30	35
Total	297	300	339	381	394

FIGURE 2:1 YEARLY SALES

Sales in year five were only three per cent up on year four, but looking at the average over the five years, the normal annual increase is about six per cent. Bearing in mind the nature of the product and the success of Marks and Spencers, it seems reasonable to assume a similar rate of growth in the future. So the historical data could be "smoothed" to give a forecast of an annual growth of six per cent for the next few years.

Looking at the monthly figures, some seasonal pattern is discernible, and in earlier years a considerable fluctuation could occur from month to month. The directors know there was a special reason for the drop in sales in the early part of year two and so it can be discounted. Moreover, they know that the levelling of monthly demand that began in years four and five is likely to continue and so the data can be "exponentially smoothed" to give additional weight to this factor. In short, an accurate forecast would be an annual growth of six per cent with relatively little fluctuation from month to month.

However, such a forecast would be based on one major assumption—namely, that Marks and Spencer would continue to buy from the firm. If the contract were terminated, this would have a catastrophic effect on the future. But it has to be taken into account in making the forecast. There must be some possibility that the contract will be ended, no matter how unlikely it seems at the time.

Prediction

If the product being sold is new to the market, there are no past records to go on. So some kind of prediction has to be made. This can range from a wild piece of wishful thinking to a very reasoned appraisal based on sophisticated market research. If it has been possible for the market research accurately to evaluate all the variables in the equation, the degree of risk will have been minimised. But some uncertainty will remain because the prediction is based on very many expressed or implied assumptions, ranging from the reliability of the research sample to the presumption that the Russians will not declare war.

Impossible Forecast Accuracy

The commercial lesson to be derived from these considerations is that it is fatal to attempt to obtain a degree of forecast accuracy that is impossible. If the best that can be done by an appraisal of the evidence is that there is a ninety-five per cent probability that sales next year will fall between £5 000 000 and £6 500 000, it is no good urging the marketing manager to "go away and work on the forecast" because it is not precise enough for the board of directors. If what is wanted is precision to the nearest £250 000, then all forecasts can accurately do is to say there is perhaps a twenty-five per cent probability of sales falling between £5 500 000 and £5 750 000. Some allowance must be made for the remote probability taking place. If the management wants to take a chance on a twenty-five per cent probability occurring, it must accept responsibility for it.

The practical effect of these matters in a distribution context is concerned with inventory decisions.

If the sales forecast is as given in Figure 2:2,

Percentage probability	Weekly sales not exceeding
95	200
50	300
5	400
0.01	500

FIGURE 2:2 SALES FORECAST

management has to decide what probabilities it can afford to cover, or afford not to cover, by inventory. If an out-of-stock situation on spare parts prejudices the sales of original equipment, it may be necessary to cover quite remote probabilities. Motor car spare stocks of twelve to eighteen months sales value are by no means unknown.

A similar situation can quite conceivably exist with many everyday products. A consumer may have a preference for a particular type of chocolate or brand of cigarette but, if the regular supplier fails to have it in stock several mornings running the consumer may try another brand instead; then there is a risk of preference for the new brand. The loss as a result of the stock failure, therefore, is not just that sale but all the future purchases the consumer would have made if he had not been induced to change his brand. This could be quite considerable.

The effect of lost sales due to an inability to supply is discussed in detail in Chapter 7.

Another important rule of probability for the sales forecaster states that if there are a number of events and they are independent, the probability of their all occurring is the product of their separate probabilities. If a coin is spun and a dice thrown, then the probability of getting heads *and* a six on the dice is:

$$\tfrac{1}{2} \times \tfrac{1}{6} = \tfrac{1}{12}$$

Translated into market terms, there might be six potential customers for an expensive machine and the probability of each of them buying might be stated as:

$$\tfrac{1}{2}, \tfrac{3}{4}, \tfrac{9}{10}, \tfrac{1}{5}, \tfrac{1}{8} \text{ and } \tfrac{1}{4}$$

The probability of all of them buying is therefore the product of all six:

$$\frac{27}{12\,800} \text{ or approximately } \frac{1}{470}$$

However, the probability of all of them *not* buying is:

$$\tfrac{1}{2} \times \tfrac{1}{4} \times \tfrac{1}{10} \times \tfrac{4}{5} \times \tfrac{7}{8} \times \tfrac{3}{4} = \frac{84}{12\,800} = \frac{1}{153}$$

The greater the number of prospects for a product, therefore, the more precise can the forecast be made.

If there is one potential customer for a £10 000 machine who is rated as being fifty per cent likely to buy, then this probability cannot be changed. There is only a fifty per cent chance he will buy and we must be guided accordingly. If, however, there are two fifty-per-cent prospects the probability that neither will buy drops to around twenty-five per cent. If there are five, the probability that none will buy drops to around three per cent. For this reason a very good way to forecast the sales of expensive units is to assign a probability of sale to each and then add them together. There might be ten potential customers for a printing machine and the likelihood of their placing orders might be expressed as in Figure 2:3.

Number of prospects ×	Percentage probability	Equal to
3	50	150
1	90	90
2	25	50
2	40	80
1	70	70
1	5	5
		445

FIGURE 2:3 FORECAST CALCULATION

From this calculation, it can be deduced that it is most likely that between four and five machines will be sold to these ten customers.

It will also be apparent that the accuracy limits of such a forecast depends on the number of prospects. If there are only two, then the forecast is much more uncertain; if there are 100 it can be accepted with considerable confidence.

The important thing is to assess and accept the degree of uncertainty that exists; a future uncertainty becomes no less uncertain because of a wish to make it so.

Danger of Underestimating

One of the dangers in forecasting is to underestimate the probabilities that exist and when it arises there is a tendency to criticise the forecaster more for failing to reach the forecast than exceeding it. If he has constructed his forecast accurately, he is not saying that the figure he presents will occur; he is saying it is more likely to occur than any other figure and that it is more and more unlikely that the actual will be farther and farther away from that figure.

A fruit machine (generally known as a "one-armed bandit") might be adjusted so that two cherries are coincident once every eight pulls on average, three oranges once every twenty-five pulls and the jackpot once every 800 pulls. But anyone who gambles with fruit machines knows perfectly well that he can put in forty coins and get nothing and yet put in one coin and get the jackpot.

The danger about a policy that judges forecasters by whether or not the forecast is exceeded is that it encourages people to underestimate "to be on the safe side". This can often be cumulative, with the forecaster keeping his figures low, with the marketing director reducing the amount to cover himself and with the managing director making an even further downward adjustment before the figures go to the board of directors. If the forecast is substantially exceeded there is a human tendency to be pleased; but the consequences of an underestimated demand can be just as unfavourable as for an overestimation.

In a situation where a number of different products are being sold, the forecasting problems depend on *how* different the products are. If they are entirely different, then the accuracy limits of the total forecast can be no finer than those for the forecasts of the individual products. If three products are sold—a pump, a gearbox and a hoist—each with a ninety per cent probability of 100 sales each year, then the probability of total sales being

300 can be no better than ninety per cent. If each of these products has a common part—say a shaft—the probability of 300 shafts being sold becomes much better than ninety per cent and the forecast for the shaft can be made much more accurately than the forecast for all these products. This fact has important consequences for the economics of component supply—a subject that is dealt with in greater detail in Chapter 8.

A logical consequence of this reasoning is that business planning should not be made entirely contingent on a particular forecast. Productive capacity can certainly be geared for optimum results on the forecast figure, but pre-planning should also make provision for coping as economically as possible with variations above and below this figure, so that the system is flexible in responding to changes in the level of demand. To say to a transport contractor that the company's requirements will be precisely x and to negotiate rates accordingly is only to lay up trouble if and when actual requirements turn out to be different. If they are below, the contractor will be demanding compensation for the capacity he has reserved; if they are above, they may only be available at premium rates. Either way, the result is to put up the unit cost of transport. Far better to ask the contractor to negotiate on the basis of requirements falling within a certain range.

The same basic reasoning applies to all the other functions—warehousing, packing, depot location and so on. If the functional managers are told to plan on the basis of future sales being at a precise specified level, their planning may not be sufficiently flexible to allow for variations about that level. If they are told to plan on the basis of sales most likely being £x but to make contingency arrangements to allow for, say, plus or minus ten per cent variations, then the firm will be in a much stronger position to withstand the vagaries of the market.

Although it is right to tackle forecasting by accurately evaluating all known data, it is wrong to underestimate the difficulties of obtaining accurate data. It is not that most market information cannot be obtained but that often it is not worth while to incur the cost to do so. Ideally, what is wanted is information on all the prospective buyers, how much will be bought next year, what the prices, costs and problems of all competitors are, and so on, and then it is simple enough to predict a sale and devise a strategy for achieving it. To obtain all this information may be possible but so costly as to exceed the total profit potential of the market. A lesser information target must be accepted and the need becomes correspondingly greater for skill and experience to be used in interpreting the data that are available.

3

The economics of transportation and delivery

"As often as a study is cultivated by narrow minds, they will draw from it narrow conclusions"

JOHN STUART MILL

There are four methods of moving goods—air, water, road and rail; each has different operating cost characteristics and each has attributes that are significant to economic distribution. The ton-mile cost (the cost of carrying one ton of cargo for one mile) is the criterion against which all transport modes are measured.

A very broad estimate of the cost of carrying a ton of goods over a distance of 100 miles is given in Figure 3:1.

Mode	Cost
Sea	30p
Rail	55p
Road	95p
Air	£11.50

FIGURE 3:1 CARRIAGE COSTS

It will be noticed that there is a well-defined correlation between the speed of each mode of transport and its cost. Although the trunking speed of rail can be higher than by road, the total elapsed time is usually greater because of terminal delays.

Referring to Figure 3:2, it will be seen that there is also a correlation between the cost of each mode of transport and the drag or resistance relative to its weight that it has to overcome when in motion.

The aeroplane has to do much more work to move itself than the others and this is the principal reason why it costs so much more. To travel 200 miles, a typical cargo aeroplane will consume four per cent of its gross weight in fuel.

Mode	Approximate specific resistance at cruising speed $\frac{\text{Resistance} \times 100}{\text{Weight}}$
Ship	0.35
Train	0.8
Truck	2.5
Aircraft	6.0

FIGURE 3:2 DRAG RESISTANCE

Payload

Since distribution transportation is used for carrying goods, an important factor is the load that can be carried in relation to the gross weight. Figure 3:3 shows the proportion of gross weight, for typical examples in the four transport modes, that can be used for payload, fuel and consumable stores.

Mode	Proportion of gross weight (%)
Ship	68
Train	51
Truck	71
Aircraft	46

FIGURE 3:3 PROPORTION OF GROSS WEIGHT

The purchase cost of a transport unit is not in itself significant. What matters is the ton-miles that can be obtained from it during its operating life and the operating costs that have to be incurred to achieve that ton-mileage.

In Figure 3:4 a comparison is made: the initial purchase cost of each transport mode and the purchase cost divided by the total ton-miles of its operating life. The second column lists the purchase cost per pound of tare weight; the third column lists the purchase cost divided by the ton-miles achieved over its working life. This shows that, although the aeroplane is in a class by itself, when it comes to purchase price relative to weight, its much higher efficiency as a transport mode shows that money invested in it gives the same order of magnitude of productivity as the train and the truck.

Mode	Purchase price (£/lb tare weight)	Purchase price (pence/capacity ton-mile)
Aircraft	30.0	0.85
Ship	0.14	0.010
Train	0.22	0.22
Truck	0.55	0.50

FIGURE 3:4 MODE PURCHASE COSTS

In terms of the productivity of the operating crews (see Figure 3:5), the aircraft is marginally superior to the ship and the train, whereas the truck is at a distinctly lower order of magnitude. This is because the operating labour/capital ratio of the truck is by far the highest of the four transport modes.

Mode	Crew productivity in ton-miles per man-hour
Aircraft	6000
Ship	5500
Train	4000
Truck	250

FIGURE 3:5 OPERATING CREW PRODUCTIVITY

The next important characteristic to consider is the rate at which ton-mile operating costs diminish with distance. It should be apparent that all forms of transport show a decreasing operating cost with increasing distance, partly because terminal costs tend to be the same, whatever the distance, and partly because many costs, such as labour and maintenance, are not directly proportional to the distance travelled.

		Cargo jet		Diesel cargo ship (displacement 1500 tons)		Diesel freight train (30 12-ton wagons)		10-ton diesel lorry	
Journey length	miles	200	2000	200	2000	200	2000	200	2000
Cruise speed	m.p.h.	590		16		55		40	
Journey speed	m.p.h.	240	540	16	16	30	30	27	17
Annual revenue Utilisation	hours	1800	3300	765	4000	2000 Locomotive 250 wagon	3300 2050	1850	5900
Direct Operating Costs pence per ton-mile									
Operating crew		0.5	0.25	0.022	0.005	0.03	0.03	0.15	0.08
Fuel and lubricants		1.1	0.50	0.011	0.009	0.02	0.02	0.27	0.27
Maintenance and materials		0.8	0.30	0.004	0.004	0.12	0.12	0.31	0.31
Depreciation		1.6	0.40	0.032	0.012	0.05	0.01	0.12	0.12
Insurance		0.5	0.12	0.035	0.013	—	—	0.05	0.02
Interest		1.0	0.25	0.032	0.012	0.05	0.02	0.04	0.02
Route and terminal costs		1.5	0.12	0.061	0.007	0.17	0.09	0.03	0.01
TOTAL DIRECT COST		7.0	1.94	0.197	0.062	0.44	0.29	0.97	0.83

FIGURE 3:6 TRANSPORT MODE OPERATING COSTS

Figure 3:6 compares in detail the operating costs of the four transport modes for distances of 200 and 2000 miles.

The largest reduction in ton-mile operating costs for the 2000-mile journey compared to the 200-mile journey is exhibited by the aircraft, followed closely by the ship. With both the aeroplane and the ship, costs fall sharply as the journey becomes longer. The main characteristic of the train is the high route and terminal costs that are involved, for both short and long journeys. The principal cost elements of the truck are fuel and maintenance and it will be noticed for that reason that the truck shows the smallest fall in operating costs of all the modes of transport as distance increases.

It is now possible to summarise the principal economic and operating attributes of the four modes of transport and it is these attributes that largely determine the proper role of each type of transport in the practice of distribution.

Aircraft

The fastest and most expensive mode of transport. Costs fall sharply as the journey becomes longer. Over long journeys, it can become directly competitive with the truck and can become more, but not directly, competitive with the train. This is because the rate of cost reduction by air over long distances is greater than by train and truck. Compared to the ship, a different situation prevails. As distance increases, the speed advantage of air becomes greater but so does its cost disadvantage, because ship-operating costs tend to decrease at a sharper rate as distance becomes longer. There are many restrictions on where an aircraft can land and many terminal delays occur which can seriously outweigh the advantage of the trunking speed.

Train

The train is limited to its permanent way. It has the highest terminal and route costs expressed as a percentage of total operating costs. Although trunking costs are low, operating problems often make the total elapsed time of moving cargo between two points unacceptably long.

Ship

The ship also has high terminal costs, which limit its competitiveness over short journeys. Over very long journeys, however, it has a cost advantage over any other mode of transport.

Truck

Operating costs are high and exceeded only by the aeroplane. However, terminal costs are low (although it can be argued that road transport does not bear its proper share of road costs) and this gives it a competitive edge over short distances. It has by far the greatest flexibility in terms of route accessibility and is therefore the most widely used medium of delivery.

Cargo transportation is only earning money when it is *en route* with a revenue-paying load. Since shippers are only paying for the transportation of their goods from one place to another, during the time a unit of transport is not moving it is not only failing to earn revenue, it is also incurring costs. This applies to loading and unloading time, maintenance time, breakdown time, time spent at base and so on. Even when a truck is locked in the garage at night, it is costing interest on the money invested in it.

Ideal Transport Mode

The ideal mode of transport, therefore, would be one that travelled for twenty-four hours a day, always travelled with a full payload, could be loaded and unloaded in a flash and required no maintenance or repair. The ideal will never be achieved but all transport operators are striving towards it—reliability, low operating costs, high crew productivity and shorter turn-round time.

A number of factors are involved and these will be examined separately.

1 *The difficulties in getting a full payload* If a scheduled service is being run, the amount of cargo offered may not be sufficient to fill the vehicle. If no scheduled service is maintained, the operator cannot hope to obtain an economic volume of business. This is a problem facing shipping lines, airlines, truck delivery services, and so on, and rates must be charged aimed at recovering costs when only a certain percentage of the payload has been reached. Again the cargo offered may not itself take up the payload but may prevent it being taken up. If, for example, a road haulier charged only on a weight basis, money would be lost if a full cargo of feathers were carried. All transportation rates, therefore, tend to take account of the weight/volume characteristics of the cargo-carrying capacity. Finally, there is the problem of multiple delivery drops. A tramp steamer calling at a succession of ports is failing to achieve optimum utility if it unloads more at each port than it takes on in new cargo.

2 *Achieving maximum utilisation* The difficulties involved in achieving utilisation around the clock are largely due to the fact that customers do not want to use the transport at an inconvenient time. Supermarket personnel do not like to receive deliveries in the middle of the night. Trains and aircraft must offer services at a time when suppliers wish to make use of them.

3 *Time limitations* This applies to the limitations in the hours that can be worked by a crew and is particularly applicable to airlines and road transport.

4 *Legislation* This will often result in operating cost increases, such as anti-pollution and noise measures, mandatory increases in the power/weight ratio of truck engines, and so on.

Cargo moves from a point of supply to a point of demand. It may be necessary, or economically desirable, to store the cargo temporarily between the points of supply and demand, but the end object is to get it to the customer, and this can involve two types of transport operations with distinctly different economic characteristics.

Trunking Movements

The first of these is the trunking movement, which can be described as the movement of a full load from one place to another. The ideal is to load to capacity the largest available transport unit (assuming that size is in inverse ratio to operating cost) and to move it as quickly as possible to its destination with the minimum crew. Post-war trends in large super-tankers, large air freighters and the insistent pressure to increase gross road vehicle weights perfectly illustrate the validity of the economic principle. A major limitation is the availability of a load to fill the transport in question. Nevertheless, all transport operators, by contracts and consolidations, are continually striving to reach the economic ideal.

However, most goods cannot be supplied by trunking movements because the amount to be delivered is well below the capacity of the transport available to deliver it. This situation can exist to some degree with a ship, aircraft or a train, but it is principally applicable to the road delivery vehicle. Important economic principles are involved and these will now be discussed in some detail. To illustrate the principles involved, it will be assumed that the supplier of the goods delivers them in his own transport.

Ideally, what the supplier would like to do is to operate the largest vehicles permitted on the road, load them to capacity and have each vehicle deliver its whole load to a single customer. In this way, the lowest cost of delivery is achieved. In practice, this cannot be done because customers are only willing to accept a smaller delivery. The supplier is therefore faced with a number of variables—how many customers are there, where are the locations and how much is required? From this, the supplier has to figure out the cheapest way to supply and this is a function of the type of vehicle used and the best way to route it.

Further analysis shows that the problem is not as straightforward as appears at first sight and to illustrate the factors that can be involved, an analysis is given in Figures 3:7, 3:8 and 3:9 of the elements of loading time, travelling time and unloading time, for the distribution of gasoline from a depot to petrol-filling stations.

Analysis of Delivery

Considering loading time, Figure 3:7, first, the tanker can be filled at the depot, either from the bottom of its tank by a pump (which is more expensive) or, filled from the top (which

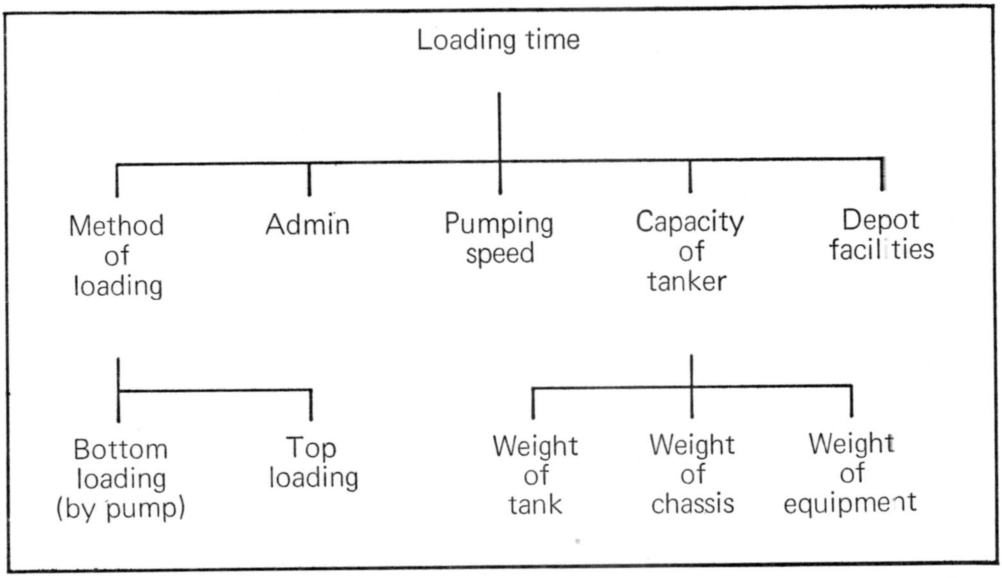

FIGURE 3:7 ANALYSIS OF FACTORS AFFECTING DELIVERY TANKER LOADING TIME

is cheaper but involves some risk of static electricity). The pumping speed is relevant as is the capacity of the tank. General facilities, such as access, speed of paper work, and other factors, can all affect the time the vehicle spends on the unproductive loading function.

Moving from the depot to the customer might seem a simple matter, but an examination of Figure 3:8 shows that many difficulties can arise. Firstly, the tanker must be routed to all customers in some logical sequence. However, this can be affected by such questions as rush-hour traffic delays, road works, acceleration of vehicle on hills, maximum speed limits, and so on. It can also be affected by whether, or not, the garage can accept deliveries outside of normal working hours and whether it is possible to control the amount delivered without running into payment difficulties.

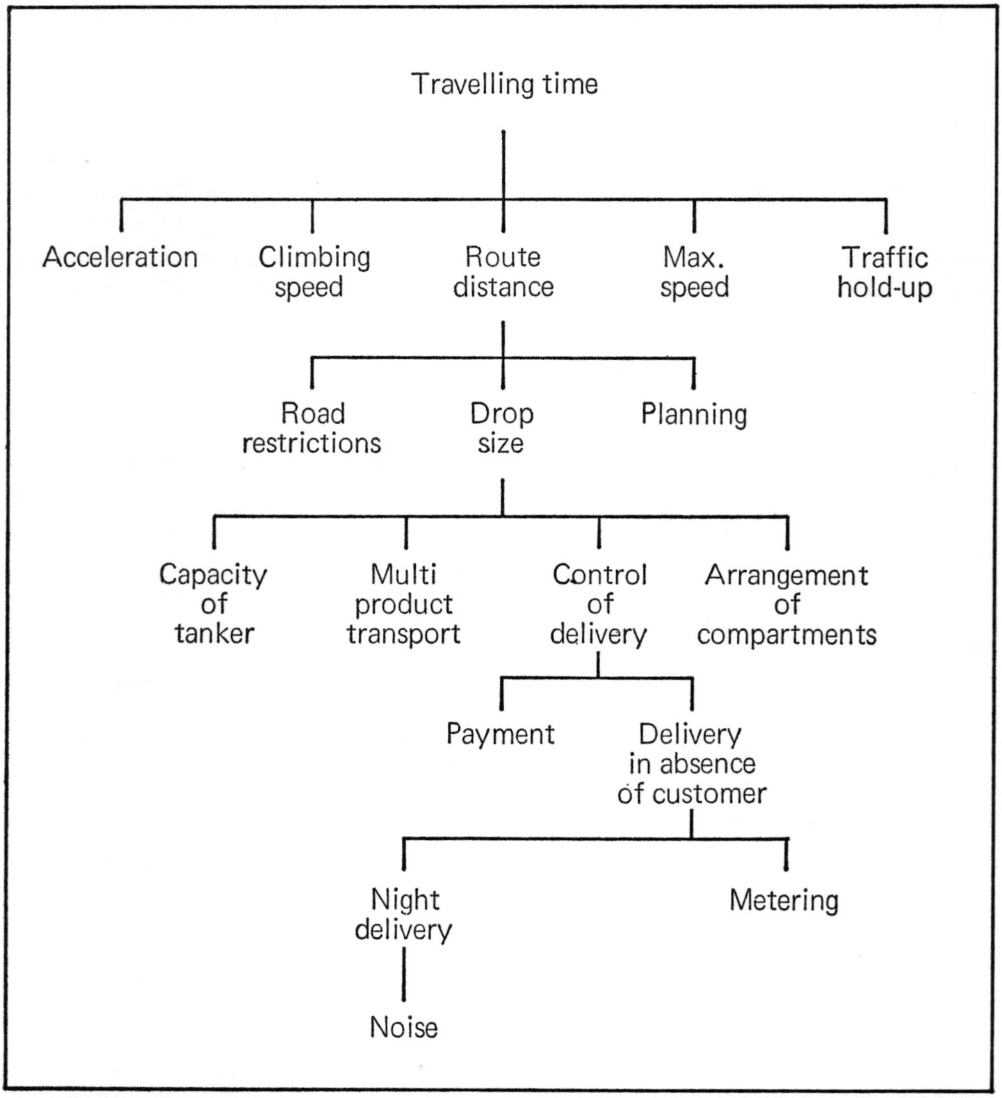

FIGURE 3:8 ANALYSIS OF FACTORS AFFECTING DELIVERY TANKER TRAVELLING TIME

Finally, there is the question of the time spent on unloading. Is access difficult for what may be the larger, more economic, vehicle? Can the oil be pumped out or must it flow by gravity? What is the size of the garage tank pipe inlet? Can two, or more, products be pumped out simultaneously?

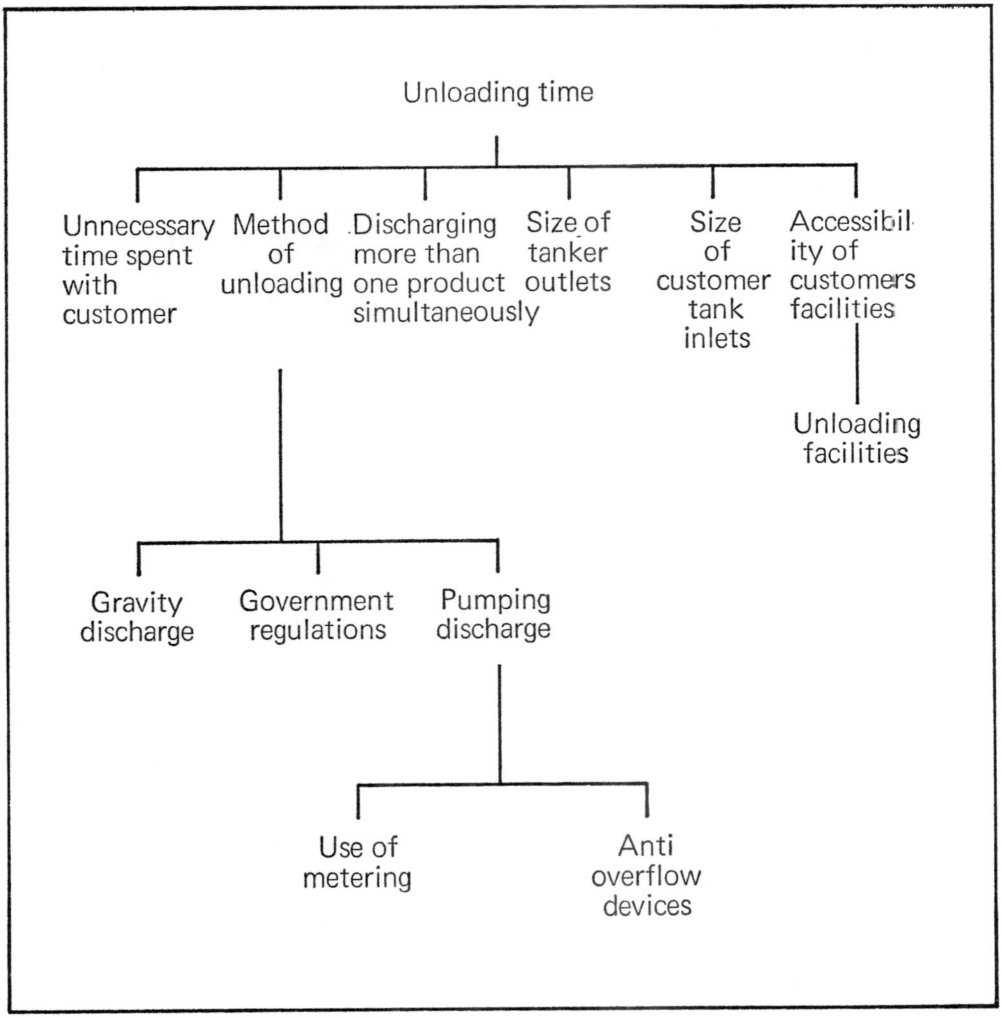

FIGURE 3:9 ANALYSIS OF FACTORS AFFECTING DELIVERY TANKER UNLOADING TIME

It is in such a situation that the economics of delivery depend to a large extent on the successful integration of all these factors. The person responsible for fitting the pieces of this jig-saw together plays an important role in the economics of distribution.

Although it is true that a road vehicle is only earning money when travelling with a revenue-paying load, it is also true that its profitability is increased if it can carry out each journey more quickly.

To continue with the example of petrol distribution, a representative analysis of the cost of running a 4000-gallon delivery vehicle, by the various elements of expenditure, is given by Figure 3:10.

Vehicle running costs	Percentage
Wages	40
Tax and insurance	5
Depreciation	17
Fuel	13
Maintenance and repairs	15
Miscellaneous	4
Tyres	6

FIGURE 3:10 VEHICLE ELEMENTS OF EXPENDITURE

The time such a vehicle spends on each activity during a twenty-four-hour day also makes informative reading, as can be seen in Figure 3:11.

Time spent	Percentage
Loading	6.5
Travelling	57.0
Unloading	12.0
Maintenance and repairs	14.0
Idle	10.5

FIGURE 3:11 VEHICLE ACTIVITY

Since the highest percentages are wages and travelling time respectively, it is clear that two ways to save money are to increase the percentage of time spent travelling and to decrease the time taken in travelling to a drop; both measures will increase the productivity of the crew.

However, the key to delivery economics lies in the size of the drop as the examples in Figure 3:12 show.

Example 1—Articulated Tanker—6600 gallons	
Number of drops	1
Distance travelled	30 miles
Discharge rate	300 gallons per minute
Cost of delivery per 100 gallons	20p
Example 2—Rigid Tanker—2000 gallons	
Number of drops	8
Distance travelled	30 miles
Discharge rate	100 gallons per minute
Cost of delivery per 100 gallons	70p

FIGURE 3:12 DELIVERY DROP ECONOMICS

Even allowing for the higher discharge rate for the larger vehicle, there is considerable economic advantage for a distributor to increase the drop size.

It is not only the size of the drop that is important. The ability of the distributor to control the size of the drop is equally significant because this makes it much easier for him to obtain the maximum utilisation from his vehicle. There will always be a tendency for the distributor to offer inducements to customers to accept a given quantity delivered at the time the distributor wishes to deliver it.

In the past, night deliveries, which seemed a logical solution to many problems, have not gained widespread acceptance largely because of the problem of the customer not having staff available to receive them. There can be little doubt, however, that the economic stimulus towards night deliveries will, in many situations, become irresistible. This will particularly apply in cities where the build-up of traffic density, if it is not controlled by legislation, will impose serious cost penalties on day deliveries.

Drop Size Economics

An important aspect of delivery economics frequently overlooked is that, over a sequence of drops, the cost of operating the vehicle is borne by a diminishing payload.

Assume, for example, the following data:

Total vehicle costs = 12p per mile
Four drops, each of three tons, at 30, 60, 90 and 120 miles from depot.

One way of calculating the true cost of delivery is to attribute the vehicle costs to the actual payload being carried as in Figure 3:13.

After given number of miles	Total cost (p)	Cost per drop (pence)			
		1	2	3	4
30	360	90	90	90	90
60	720		120	120	120
90	1080			180	180
120	1440				360
Actual cost		90	210	390	750
Ton-mile cost		1	1.17	1.44	2.08

FIGURE 3:13 VEHICLE PAYLOAD MILEAGE COSTS

This is a perfectly valid, and indeed strictly true, method of apportioning the costs rather than by dividing the total cost by four drops and concluding that it is 360 pence per drop.

To approach delivery costs from this standpoint might very well reveal significant information regarding the question of using hired transport rather than owned transport. It is not difficult to believe that, in the example given in Figure 3:13, it may prove cheaper to revise the delivery schedules so that drop four is given to an outside carrier.

In practice, of course, a compromise must be reached with the true economic situation because there is no economic alternative to using vehicles for apparently uneconomic drops. This is because the vehicle would then become idle and would accumulate labour and depreciation charges.

Unit Loads

It will be clear that, because of the development of containers, pallets and other units, loading becomes more economic because these methods decrease the time during which transport modes are unproductive. A freight container consigned from London to Sydney might travel on a truck, train, ship and an aeroplane. Not only is the loading and unloading process quicker, if the shape of the container is compatible with the shape of the transport unit, better use is made of the cargo space available. Demountable vans, swop body and articulated vehicles are all examples of the application of this economic principle.

How to Determine Delivery Costs

To enable the reader to determine delivery costs in a practical way, a delivery cost analysis example is shown in Figure 3:14. Notes are supplied to enable the correct details to be compiled in the analysis.

DELIVERY COSTS	£ Total cost per period
Vehicle operating costs Loading costs Unloading costs Dispatch and documentation costs	
Total delivery costs over period	£
Number of delivery drops in period	____________
Cost per delivery drop	____________

FIGURE 3:14 DELIVERY COST ANALYSIS

Notes:

1 Vehicle operating costs include depreciation, maintenance, fuel, tax, insurance and wages.

2 Loading and unloading costs include labour costs, excluding vehicle personnel, and rent or, depreciation on any special equipment.

3 Dispatch and documentation include all office costs associated with vehicle scheduling, dispatch, office records, and so on.

4 By dividing the number of units delivered to any delivery point by the total number of deliveries to that point, multiplied by the average cost per delivery drop, some indication can be gained as to the profitability of individual deliveries.

4

The economics of holding stock

"Irrationally held truths may be more harmful than reasoned errors"
THOMAS HENRY HUXLEY

Storing a product costs money. Costs have been incurred in producing the product and getting it into store and costs are now being incurred in storing it. In general, these expenses are not recovered until the product is sold and paid for and it is therefore in the interests of everyone that it should remain in store for as short a time as possible.

The cost constituents of holding stock can be summarised as follows:

Cost of building
Cost of utilities
Cost of handling and storage equipment
Taxes, if any
Wages
Administration and office expenses

Cost of product deterioration whilst in store
Cost of product obsolescence whilst in store
Interest on money invested in the product being stored.

In general, it can be said that the costs above the line rarely amount to more than about five per cent of the product value and since these are the costs that tend to be classified in the accounts, and therefore to be most subject to scrutiny by management, there is a real danger of ignoring or underestimating the three costs that lie below the line.

When a product goes into store, it nearly always has a selling price ascribed to it, and this price is based on the market situation at the time of going into store and represents the seller's expectation of what the market will pay for it at that time. During the time the product is in storage, two things can happen to depreciate the selling price:

1 The product suffers some form of physical damage or deterioration and the buyer will only take it at a reduced price. Shop-soiled garments, consumer durables that have been dented or scratched are examples. Therefore, a cost has to be incurred either in restoring the article to its original condition or in accepting a lower price from the customer.

2 The product becomes obsolescent during its time in storage and the selling price ascribed to it when it first went into store can no longer be obtained. Last year's fashions are an obvious example of obsolescence but other examples are not quite so obvious. If a competitor produces a better piece of equipment, in terms of price or application, than the one in store, then the latter may have to stand a price reduction. If it is now less effective than the competitor's in terms of application, it may even be unsaleable or it may have to be left in store much longer before it can be moved. All these are examples of costs caused by obsolescence.

The cost of interest on the money already spent on the product when it goes into store varies according to the situation of the firm that has invested the money—how much does money cost on the market, how difficult is it to get and what can be earned on it? The true cost of interest can therefore vary from, say, five per cent to twenty-five per cent and it is a cost that has to be determined by each company in the light of its own circumstances.

The point to emphasise is that these three costs, interest, deterioration and obsolescence, nearly always greatly exceed the costs of operating the warehouse and therefore the greatest scope for cost reduction lies in reducing the size of the inventory. Since inventory must fulfil a purpose, it is essential to understand the purpose in order to judge what the optimum size of the stock level should be. There are three basic reasons for holding stock and they will be considered separately. The first is to permit the most economic form of production, the second is to protect against uncertainty about the time it takes to replenish the stock and the third is to protect against uncertainty about when and how much the customer will buy.

Production Stock

Batch production unit costs

Size of batch	Unit cost (£)
10	50
20	49
30	48
40	46
50	44
60	41

Stock-holding costs = 20%
Annual demand = 360 units

FIGURE 4:1 PRODUCTION VERSUS STOCK ECONOMICS

If demand is uneven, as it usually is, it hardly ever pays to manufacture at the corresponding rate when a continuous production process is involved. Even if demand is highly seasonal, as with fireworks or Christmas gifts, it is still usually more economic to spread production out over a longer period. To do this, however, involves the accumulation of stock and this cost has to be compared to the lower cost of production. A simple example is given in Figure 4:1. Unit production costs are at their lowest when monthly output is evened out throughout the year (as in Figure 4:2, Example A) and, because demand is seasonal, there is a significant build-up of stock during the off-season months. On a continuous production process, it is difficult to envisage a more economic solution to the satisfaction of demand and it will invariably pay to hold the stock.

Month	Demand	Production	Stock
1	10	30	100
2	10	30	120
3	20	30	130
4	40	30	120
5	100	30	50
6	60	30	20
7	50	30	Nil
8	30	30	Nil
9	10	30	20
10	10	30	40
11	10	30	60
12	10	30	80
			Average = 62

FIGURE 4:2 EXAMPLE A

Month	Demand	Production	Total cost (£)	Stock
1	10	20	980	10
2	10	20	980	20
3	20	20	980	20
4	40	60	2460	40
5	100	60	2460	Nil
6	60	60	2460	Nil
7	50	60	2460	10
8	30	20	980	Nil
9	10	10	500	Nil
10	10	10	500	Nil
11	10	10	500	Nil
12	10	10	500	Nil
		Averages =	15 750	8

FIGURE 4:3 EXAMPLE B

It will be seen that with a continuous production process, example *A* (see Figure 4:2) would almost certainly be the cheaper alternative, in spite of the higher stock cost.

With a batch production process, example *A* would give production costs of £17 280 plus stock holding costs (at 20%) of £600 = £17 880. Example *B* (see Figure 4:3) would give production costs of £15 760 plus stock-holding costs of about £80 = £15 840.

In a multi-product plant, different products can be manufactured, but only one at a time. Stocks of each product will have to be maintained to satisfy demand until capacity can be allocated to its production. This is another example of using stocks to achieve the most economic balance of manufacture.

On a batch production basis, manufacturing economics can change, partly because unit costs drop as the size of the batch increases and partly because it is often practicable to sub-contract work during peak periods. Using the batch production costs given in Figure 4:1, the annual cost of production would be £17 280 plus a stock-holding cost of some £600 (see Figure 4:2, example *A*). If, however, the size of the batches is varied relative to the state of demand (see Figure 4:3, example *B*) production costs drop to £15 760 and there is also a considerable decrease in the average stock level.

The second reason for holding stock is protection against uncertainty of supply. A manufacturer will stock raw materials so that he will not have to close the factory if his supplier lets him down. A warehouse manager will build in protection against the possibility that the ship bringing goods may be delayed, or that some may be lost or damaged. If the consignee is not absolutely sure of getting exactly what he wants, exactly when he wants it, he will want to have a safety reserve. The way consumers hoard a product when it becomes scarce is an everyday illustration of the same principle. The reason being that there is an uncertainty about the future supply position.

Work-in-progress is not regarded as a stock in this context. However, problems do arise when different processes have to be carried out to the same product, or if different components are required for a single assembly. These problems are considered in detail in Chapter 8.

Demand Stock

The third reason for holding stock is to cover uncertainty in demand. If demand is known beforehand, there is no need for a stock contingency and the only function of stock would be to optimise the economics of production or protect against uncertainty in lead time. It will be noted that the stock levels given in Figure 4:1 are only just large enough to meet the monthly variation in demand. In practice, a further stock reserve would have to be held to protect against the possibility of less favourable variations in the monthly level of demand.

The average amount of stock that is held will depend, in the main, on three considerations:

1 *The order quantity* The larger this is, the higher the average stock will be. The size of the most economic order quantity will depend on production economics or buying terms (depending on whether the order is placed "in-house" or with an outside supplier) and the cost of placing the order.

2 *The replenishment lead time* This is the total time that elapses between the placing of the stock replenishment order and the receipt of the goods. Again, the longer the lead time, the higher the average stock level will be, especially in-transit stock. If re-ordering is done against a re-order point, the numerical size of the re-order point will be in direct proportion to the length of the lead time.

3 *The amount of safety stock.* This will depend on the level of service given and on the frequency distribution of demand, which is a way of describing the extent to which weekly demand can rise above, or fall below, the weekly average.

Reduction of Stock Level

If it is true that the principal burden of inventory lies in the money invested in the stock, then the major scope for economy lies in reducing the average stock level. There are two ways of doing this. One is to accept a lower level of service—which means that stocks will become exhausted more often; and the other is to reduce the replenishment lead time, which will permit the same level of in-stock reliability with a lower average inventory.

To consider first the acceptability of a lower level of service, it has first to be decided what the economic consequences will be. One favourable consequence is to lower the investment in stock and this is a saving that can be measured. The possible unfavourable consequences, on the other hand, are not so easy to measure. A significant factor is whether, or not, a customer, finding the item out of stock, is prepared to await delivery or turn to another source of supply. It is easy enough to obtain opinion about what the customer will do in these circumstances but it is not so simple to obtain hard fact. In certain circumstances it might be possible to carry out controlled experiments. Firstly, find out how serious the initial demand was and then follow up on the action the customer takes when told the item is out of stock. Does the customer wait, or buy a substitute or a competitive product, perhaps a purchase is not made at all, and so on? This may appear an unnecessary complication, but one has only to consider the purchase of a marginal labour-saving device for the kitchen to see that the customer's reaction could be extremely difficult to determine.

Another factor is whether or not the stock-out will have more serious long-term economic consequences than the loss of that particular sale. If a customer, finding the product out of stock, then buys a competitive product instead, some danger will exist that he will continue to buy the competitive product either because, having tried it, he finds he likes it better, or because the availability of the competitive product has subconsciously affected his buying habits. It is almost impossible to form definite conclusions about a customer's buying habits in this respect but some sensible assumptions can be made depending on the product. For example, the loss of an order of a typewriter from a housewife is only likely to connote the loss of profit on that particular sale. The loss of an order to a large company, on the other hand, who, as a result of the failure to supply, buys from another supplier for the next five years, can be considerable.

In Figure 4:4, let it be assumed that the cost of each typewriter is £100 and that stock-holding costs are twenty per cent.

Average stock level		Stock-holding costs @ 20% (£)
Number of typewriters	Value (£)	
100	10 000	2000
80	8 000	1600
60	6 000	1200

FIGURE 4:4 STOCK REDUCTION COSTS

A reduction in stock of twenty typewriters will save £400 a year. If this resulted in a stock-out only twenty times a year and profit on each machine was ten per cent, then the reduction would appear to be justified. The stock saving of £400 is, on the face of it, better than the £200 loss in profit on the assumption that each stock-out resulted in the loss of one machine order. But suppose that, as a result of one of these stock-outs, a large customer switches brands and buys fifty typewriters over the next two years from another firm. The true profit loss on such an assumption is £500 and this does not justify even by itself an average stock reduction of twenty machines.

Now it can rarely, if ever, be known what these long-term consequences of a stock-out might be. But common sense would suggest trying to avoid running out of stock to large customers and it is therefore essential to make some reasonable assumptions on these possibilities in determining what sort of stock investment to have. It has been suggested that if British car manufacturers had invested more money and to better effect in spare parts stocks in the USA in the nineteen-fifties they would not have suffered such a large reduction in their share of that country's car market, with a correspondingly adverse effect on their profit level. If it is appropriate to consider the loss of business not in terms of the net profit loss but in terms of the lost contribution, it is conceivable that the consequences of stock-outs can be even more serious.

It would be wrong to underestimate the difficulties involved in obtaining accurate information about the effect of stock-outs. The proprietor of a retail shop will tend to stock up on lines for which he is asked. In larger establishments, it would be necessary to record every instance of stock-out—something that employees are not used to doing—and then attempt to draw some significant conclusions from the record. As with all unfamiliar notions, it would be only too easy to surrender to the difficulties.

None the less, the dangers of ignoring these matters cannot be over-emphasised. Expenditure on stocks must be justified. It is foolish to develop pre-conceived notions about what this expenditure ought to be. Even though it is impossible to make precise calculations about the economic effects of increasing or decreasing inventory, some order of magnitude must be established. Stock is not a liability; it is a vital tool in the determination of long-term profit.

Stock Definition

If stock is defined as investment in unsold goods then it is clear that stock does not have to be in a warehouse. If it is paid for, but not yet sold, then it is a stock investment, whether it is on the quayside, in a ship, in an aeroplane or on a truck. Therefore, at any given time, inventory consists of:

1 Goods paid for and stored in the warehouse
2 Goods ordered and paid for and not yet received
3 Goods despatched but not yet paid for

If goods are ordered and in transit but not paid for, then the interest cost is being borne by the consignor. Who bears the other costs depends on the contract of sale and this will depend on whether the goods are ex-factory, FOB, CIF, delivered etc. If goods are dispatched but not yet paid for, the position is reversed. This is an important distinction to bear in mind because the amount of goods ordered and in the course of delivery can often exceed the actual level of those goods stored in the warehouse; and it is costing somebody money.

Starting stock—400 units
Replenishment lead time—4 weeks
Order quantity—40 units

End of week	Demand	Orders placed	Goods received	Stock balance
1	100	—	—	300
2	100	—	—	200
3	100	—	—	100
4	100	400	400	400
5	100	—	—	300
6	100	—	—	200
7	100	—	—	100
8	100	400	400	400

FIGURE 4:5 CONSTANT DEMAND

Figure 4:5 portrays a situation (in practice hardly ever achieved) where demand is constant. Sales are always 100 units every week. At the beginning of each 4-week period there are 400 units in stock. After one week, the stock drops to 300, after two weeks to 200, after three weeks to 100 and after four weeks to zero. Then in come another 400 units into stock and the cycle starts again. Clearly, the average stock investment in this situation is:

$$\frac{400 + 300 + 200 + 100}{4} = 200 \text{ units}$$

If the amount ordered each time is reduced from 400 to 200, so that a supply comes in every two weeks instead of every four, then the average stock level will be halved—see Figure 4:6. The less the order quantity, the lower the average stock. But this saving has to be weighed against the increased ordering costs and also probably the higher unit cost of the goods being bought because they are being purchased in smaller quantities. In any situation there is an economic order quantity, and the factors that affect this are described in detail in an appendix near the end of the book.

End of week	Demand	Orders placed	Goods received	Stock balance
1	100	—	—	10
2	100	200	200	20
3	100	—	—	10
4	100	200	200	20
5	100	—	—	10
6	100	200	200	20
7	100	—	—	10
8	100	200	200	20

FIGURE 4:6 HALVING THE ORDER

It will be noticed that no effect will be made on the average stock level in the warehouse by reducing lead time. It does not matter what the lead time is; if demand is known and constant, then advance orders can be placed to meet that demand and the average stock level will remain the same unless the order quantity is changed. This is not so with intransit stock, of course, which is directly affected by the length of lead time.

In practice, demand is never constant; it varies from week to week. Moreover, it is impossible to know beforehand what the degree of variation is going to be. It may be possible to affirm that it is unlikely to go above a given level or fall below another level. It may even be possible to draw some conclusions from historical data about the frequency of the demand variation, as in Figure 4:7, when demand averages 100 units a week over a fifty-week period but can vary.

Weeks ×	Units	Total
2	140	280
3	130	390
10	120	1200
20	100	2000
10	80	800
3	70	210
2	60	120
		5000

FIGURE 4:7 DEMAND VARIATION

Safety Stock

Comparing Figure 4:7 with Figure 4:5, the difference is between certain demand and uncertain demand. In Figure 4:5, it is known beforehand that demand is going to be 100 units a week. In Figure 4:7 all that is known is that weekly demand could range anywhere between sixty and 140 units. In order to satisfy such unpredictability of demand, it can be demonstrated that some additional stock must be held, over and above the average stock level of Figure 4:5, that is a function of the order quantity used. This additional stock is described as a safety or buffer stock. How much it should be depends on the level of service it is intended to give to the customer. If it is intended to give a 100 per cent level of service then the safety stock will have to be sufficient to meet the highest possible level of demand which, over the lead time period of four weeks, is two weeks at 140 units a week and two weeks at 130 units. It would have to total 140 units (40 + 40 + 30 + 30) effectively, everything over and above 100 units a week.

Only in very rare circumstances, when it was necessary to guard against the most unlikely contingencies, would a 100% level of in-stock reliability be justified. The odds against demand in a four-week period in Figure 4:7 totalling 540 units are about 175 000:1 and it is such a remote probability that the normal business would not be justified in holding stock to cover it. They would very likely settle on a solution that would give, say, a ninety-five per cent in-stock reliability.

It will be clear, therefore, that the level of demand safety stock will depend not only on the level of service it is desired to give but also on the frequency distribution of demand itself. If, as shown in Figure 4:7, maximum demand never rose above 120 units a week instead of 140 (when average weekly demand is 100) then the amount of safety stock required would be considerably less.

In the Appendix, models have been constructed on a normal frequency distribution of demand to determine the exact amount of safety stock that is required for a given lead time and this demonstrates the truth that a reduction in lead time, although it has no affect on the average inventory level needed to service average demand, does reduce the amount of safety stock required for the same level of service.

The results, comparing lead times of six weeks and three weeks, can be summarised as in Figure 4:8.

	Lead time 6 weeks	Lead time 3 weeks
	Units	Units
Economic order quantity	350	350
Average stock level in warehouse	354	263
Average stock level in transit	528	273
Minimum safety stock required to avoid stock-out	100	50

FIGURE 4:8 COMPARISON OF LEAD TIMES

In this situation, therefore, a reduction in replenishment lead time from six to three weeks results in a reduction in warehouse stock of almost twenty-six per cent, a reduction of in-transit stock of over forty-eight per cent and a reduction in safety stock of fifty per cent.

Therefore, reducing lead time from six to three weeks does not, in all circumstances, result in similar stock reductions. The amount of reduction depends on two variables:

1 *The Order Quantity* The larger this is for the same level of demand, the higher the average stock level will be, both in the warehouse and in transit.

1 *The Frequency Distribution of Demand* The higher demand in any particular period can rise above the average for all periods, the greater the amount of safety stock is needed to give the same level of service and the greater the reduction of safety stock that can be obtained from a shorter lead time.

How to Determine the Cost of Holding Stock

	Annual cost (£)
Rent or depreciation on building	
Utilities (gas, water, electricity, heating)	
Depreciation on equipment used in building	
Wages and salaries	
Administration expenses	
Taxes	
Other operating costs (if any)	
Total annual operating cost	

FIGURE 4:9 COST OF HOLDING STOCK

The costs listed in Figure 4:9 are not directly proportional to the volume of stock. Very significant changes in the amount of stock in a given building can obviously have effect on the cost of wages, utilities and administration, but, in general, the changes involved will not be large.

The costs that are directly proportional to the amount of stock are:

1 *Obsolescence* This has to be estimated as a percentage cost, either on the basis of past experience and/or on the basis of any expectation that there will be a particular obsolescence risk arising in the future. For example, some obsolescence risk always applies to women's skirts, related to colour, style and so on, but if there were a future possibility of skirts going completely out of fashion, to be replaced by trousers, then account would have to be taken of this special obsolescence risk.

2 *Deterioration* Exactly the same factors apply to deterioration as to obsolescence, except that deterioration refers to a physical change in the product—damage, dirt, rust etc —that lowers its value.

3 *Interest on money invested in stock* Again, this is a percentage cost and has to be determined by management in accordance with the value the company places on money.

Obsolescence—1%
Deterioration—2%
Money invested—15%

	Value (£)		
	(1)	(2)	(3)
Average stock value	100 000	130 000	170 000
Operating cost, say	5 000	5 000	6 000
Obsolescence	1 000	1 300	1 700
Deterioration	2 000	2 600	3 400
Money investment	15 000	19 500	25 500
Annual stock-holding cost	23 000	28 400	36 600
Percentage	23	21.8	21.6

FIGURE 4:10 COSTS DIRECTLY PROPORTIONAL TO STOCK

How to Determine the Most Economic Quantity of Demand Stock

1 Estimate *average* weekly or monthly demand. This can either be based on past experience, modified where necessary in the light of changing circumstances; or it can be a prediction based on what is expected to happen. __________

2 Estimate *maximum* weekly or monthly demand and the frequency with which demand is going to rise to or near the maximum.

Maximum __________

Number of weeks or months __________

3 Calculate the *average* demand stock, which is half the economic order quantity (see Figure 4:6) __________

4 Add a safety stock of half the difference between average weekly demand and maximum weekly demand multiplied by the number of weeks in a year it is expected to be at or near the maximum.

Average unit weekly demand	2 000
Maximum unit weekly demand	3 000
Number of *weeks* in year demand is expected to be at or or near maximum	6
Economic order quantity of units	10 000
∴ Average demand stock (half the EOQ)	5 000
Safety stock [half the difference between 2000 and 3000 units multiplied by the number of weeks demand is at or near maximum (500 × 6)]	3 000
	8 000

FIGURE 4:11 EXAMPLE OF ECONOMIC QUANTITY OF DEMAND STOCK

It should be borne in mind that this method of calculating safety stock is unsophisticated and, although it will give satisfactory results in most instances, it assumes a fairly regular variation of weekly demand above or below the average. Where the maximum demand is much above the average and yet occurs only infrequently, this method might tend to understate the amount of safety stock required for any given level of customer service.

Determination of Economic Order Quantity

Formulae can be constructed for this purpose as described in the appendix, but the examples shown in Figures 4:12 and 4:13 illustrate arithmetically how the economic order quantity (EOQ) can be determined.

It is assumed, in Figure 4:12, that a certain product costs £1 for 100 units (1p per unit) if ordered in quantities of 10 000 units or more. For smaller quantities, an additional price per 100 units is charged.

Order quantity	Additional price per 100 units (pence)
70 000–99 999	1
50 000–69 999	2
35 000–49 999	4
20 000–34 999	6
10 000–19 999	12

FIGURE 4:12 PURCHASING COST

The factors that have to be taken into account are as follows:

The quantity price —see Figure 4:12
Annual requirements —700 000 units
Stock-holding cost —15%
Marginal cost of an order—£1.25

The factors are dealt with in Figure 4:13.

Order quantity	Price per 100 units	Annual number of orders	Annual cost (£)			
			Material	Stock holding	Ordering	Total
10 000	1.12	70	7840	8	87	7935
19 999	1.12	35	7840	17	44	7901
20 000	1.06	35	7420	16	44	7480
34 999	1.06	20	7420	28	25	7473
35 000	1.04	20	7280	27	25	7332
49 999	1.04	14	7280	39	18	7337
50 000	1.02	14	7140	39	18	7197
69 999	1.02	10	7140	53	13	7206
70 000	1.01	10	7070	53	13	7136
99 999	1.01	7	7070	76	9	7155
100 000	1.00	7	7000	76	9	7085
140 000	1.00	5	7000	105	6	7111

FIGURE 4:13 ECONOMIC ORDER QUANTITY

The economic order quantity therefore is 100 000 units.

How to Determine the Economic Order Balance

(a)	(b)	(c)	(d)	(e)	(f)	(g)	(h)	(i)
Order quantity	Number of orders	Price per unit	Annual usage in units	Annual purchasing cost	Average stock level	Annual stock holding cost	Cost of placing orders	Total annual cost

FIGURE 4:14 HOW TO DETERMINE THE ECONOMIC BALANCE

The use of Figure 4:14 will determine the most economic balance between the cost of placing orders, the cost of holding stock and the purchasing cost where the unit purchase cost varies according to the quantity ordered.

1 In Figure 4:14, columns (a) to (e) inclusive summarise the different costs of purchase according to the quantity discounts involved.
2 The stock-holding cost, columns (f) to (g), is a function of the average amount of stock in the warehouse (and in transit, if the in-transit stock is paid for) and the percentage cost of holding stock which is calculated in accordance with the guide given by Figure 4:10. If, for example, the average quantity of material in stock has a value of £100 000 and the percentage cost of holding stock is twenty per cent, then the figure that goes in column (g) is £20 000.
3 Estimate the cost of placing a single order (see Figure 4:13) and multiply this by the number of orders placed in column (b) to give the figure in column (h).
4 Add columns (e), (g) and (h) to give the total annual cost in column (i). The lowest total in column (i) will correspond with the most economic order quantity in column (a).

5

The economics of air freight

Cecil Graham: "What is a cynic?"
Lord Darlington: "A man who knows the price of everything and the value of nothing"

OSCAR WILDE, *Lady Windermere's Fan, Act III*

Air freight is given a separate chapter in this book because it is becoming an increasingly important aspect of distribution. It must be appreciated, however, that what air freight permits is a reduction in supply lead times, and the economic consequences of a reduced lead time by any other means would be exactly the same.

Lead time is not synonymous with transit time. From an economic standpoint, the significance is in the total lead time, the period between deciding to place the order and subsequently receiving the goods. This comprises the time taken to place the order, to get it to the source of supply, to process the order, to handle the goods, to transport them and any time *en route* during which they are in store. A train, for example, can usually travel between two points faster than a truck; but the total lead time by train will often be much longer than by truck because it involves longer terminal delays, trans-shipment from truck to train and back to truck at the other end and so on.

By the same token, the advantages of air freight can be severely eroded by clearance delays. There seems little point in air-freighting something out to Teheran in five hours, if it is then going to languish at the airport for two weeks waiting for the consignee to come and take it away.

Air freight competes with all forms of surface transport, but in particular it competes with sea transport because it is mainly between distant overseas countries that the chief scope for the use of air freight exists. In fact, it first began to assume economic importance in the large land mass of the USA but there is little doubt that its future growth lies in overseas trade.

There are two approaches to the question of air freight. One, is to compare the overall cost of shipping by sea and air between the point of origin and the final points of destination. This was the approach much beloved by airlines in the early days of selling air freight and it exploited the superior handling methods of the airlines. A typical "cost comparison" presented by the air cargo salesman to a customer would read as follows:

	SEA (£)	AIR (£)
Freight rate	500	1000
Packing	400	20
Insurance	80	20
Inland transport	120	70
Interest on money invested in goods in transit at six per cent	90	10
	1190	1120

What was happening in this comparison was that the higher cost of the air freight bill was largely being offset by the lower cost of packing by air. There was no real reason why the packing cost had to be so much higher by sea; a shipping line could handle goods just as well as airlines if it had to; and by using freight containers and container ships, it did in fact begin to do this during the nineteen-sixties.

Inherent Advantages

It is important to distinguish between the inherent advantages of air freight—those with which other modes of transport cannot compete—and the advantages it may temporarily have because of shortcomings by other modes of transport. The only inherent advantage that air freight has is *speed.* It can get the goods there far more quickly than any other form of transport can hope to do. However, this speed can only be achieved at a higher cost because, within the existing limits of technological knowledge, it is inconceivable that the ton-miles cost of air freight will ever come near to that of surface transport.

As a very broad estimate, the cost of carrying a ton of goods 100 miles is about forty times greater by air than by sea. The differential between air and surface transport is unbridgeable. It will always cost significantly more to send goods by air freight.

But the operating cost of transport is not the only criterion. Equally important for the economics of air freight is the different weight/volume ratios of the different transport units and any distinctions that may exist in the rating methods of the operators.

The following shows the carrying capabilities per cubic foot of available cargo space for the four modes of transport:

	Pounds per cubic foot
Large cargo jet	10.9
12-ton truck	22.3
12-ton railway wagon	29.8
Cargo ship of 15 000 tons displacement	40.9

These characteristics are reflected in the rating structure, because shippers usually charge for one ton or forty cubic feet, whichever is the greater. A sea shipment has to have a very high weight density of fifty-six pounds per cubic foot or more to avoid paying on volume.

Airlines basically charge on weight, although they do apply a volume charge when the density drops below ten pounds per cubic foot.

It follows, therefore, that in the comparative economics of shipping cargo by sea or air, the rate differential drops in inverse ratio to the density of the cargo.

If, for example, a comparison is made on a one-ton shipment between a transatlantic rate of £20 per ton weight measurement by sea and £0.25 per kilo by air, the following freight bill for the different densities is seen:

Density (lbs/cu. ft)	Cost by sea (£)	Cost by air (£)	Cost differential (£)
10	112	250	138
20	56	250	194
30	37.35	250	212.65
40	28	250	222
50	22.40	250	227.60
60	18.60	250	231.40

Freight rate—Sea £20 per ton weight measurement
Air 25p per kilo

FIGURE 5:1 FREIGHT COMPARISONS

This has important consequences for air freight because, in general, the low, density cargoes' where the air to sea rate differential is as its lowest, are usually cargoes with a high value weight ratio—shoes and machinery are two examples.

In spite of the fact that air freight becomes more favourable from a rating standpoint as the density drops, a small differential will, in practice, always exist. Although there are one or two freak instances where a high *ad valorem* rate by sea will actually result in a lower rate by air, for the purpose of distribution economics it can be assumed that there will always be a differential.

Since a consignor will not pay more for air freight without good economic reason, the function of air freight economics must be to define and measure these reasons.

The first and obvious reason is one of emergency—a drilling rig lying idle in the desert at a cost of £1000 a day for lack of a drilling bit, a child dying in a distant place for lack of a particular medicine. In such emergencies, cost is not a significant criterion.

There is a second but diminished category of emergency where cost does become significant—an example being the exporter who, being late with delivery, is willing to pay something more in higher transport charges to satisfy the customer. This imposes a limit beyond which the exporter cannot afford to go.

If emergency consignments are excluded—and it is worth remembering that at one time they accounted for virtually all air cargo and even today account for a high proportion of it—the only use for air freight is as a tool of distribution.

Air Freight Method of Distribution

Experience shows that there are in fact only four justifications for spending more to send goods by air.

1 Money is invested in the cargo for a shorter period of time by virtue of the shorter transit time
2 The insurer is at risk for a shorter period of time, which would normally reduce the premium paid. Note that any reduction in premium for air consignments as a consequence of less propensity to damage is not an inherent advantage of the speed of air. Ships can compete in this area if they want to or need to
3 It results in a sale that could otherwise not have taken place
This can be further sub-divided into three situations:
(a) The cargo is perishable or subject to obsolescence and cannot survive the surface journey without losing value
(b) The customer will only buy if the commodity is obtainable within a period that is too short for a sea journey. In general, this only applies to custom-built products
(c) A commodity to be rented can earn rent sooner if it gets there faster
4 It lowers the cost of storage and distribution in the country of sale

Point four often offers the best scope for justifying air freight, but it is a somewhat complex situation and requires further discussion.

The only true economic effect of a reduced lead time on inventories is to reduce the stock required to service a given level of demand. From the standpoint of servicing minimum or average demand, it does not matter how long the lead time is provided demand can be forecast ahead over the length of lead time and provided the length of lead time does not result in deterioration or obsolescence of the goods. If some minimum level of demand can be foreseen, this can be supplied by surface transport, no matter how long it takes.

The extent to which demand will rise at any time above this minimum is uncertain and the uncertainty can be insured against by holding safety stock in the country of sale. The amount of safety stock will depend on the level of service it is desired to give.

It must be appreciated that a reduction in lead time affects only the amount of safety stock held in the warehouse. It has no effect on the stock level required to service a minimum or average demand. If it is assumed that demand is exactly 100 units per week, that the lead time is three weeks and the economic order quantity is 300 units, then every three weeks, when stocks have just reached zero, a fresh consignment of 300 units will arrive and will be subsequently consumed during the following three-week period. In these circumstances, the average warehouse stock level will always be 150 units no matter how long the lead time. This applies only to stock held in the warehouse; in-transit stock, is, of course, affected by the length of lead time.

As soon as any degree of uncertainty is introduced into the situation, whether this is concerned with the length of lead time or the level of demand, then a safety or buffer stock must be added to the average stock level in order to safeguard against the uncertainty.

It can be demonstrated that, the farther ahead one tries to forecast sales, the less reliable the forecast becomes. Therefore, the longer the replenishment lead time, the more safety stock is required to give a defined level of service. It is in this context that the use of air freight in stock reduction becomes relevant. To the extent that it reduces the replenishment lead time, it permits a reduction in safety stock for any given level of service.

An important factor in this regard is the frequency distribution of demand, in other words, the extent to which demand is distributed about its mean. If a situation exists whereby demand can rise considerably above the mean at infrequent intervals—to put it into technical language, the frequency demand curve has a positive skew—then the amount of safety stock needed to cover, say, a ninety-eight per cent in-stock reliability is considerably greater than if demand never rises very much above the mean. This is the economic characteristic of a spare parts market. A particular spare may be demanded very infrequently but its unavailability can have serious consequences on original equipment sales. In these circumstances, high safety stocks are common and these can be quite significantly reduced by a shorter lead time.

Part Air Consignments

Further analysis shows that it is not necessary to cut lead time on all consignments in order to effect significant stock reductions. If a conceptual distinction is made between stock required to service average demand and stock required to service above-average demand, it has already been shown that the former is not affected by the length of lead time. It is therefore not necessary, from a purely inventory standpoint, to use air freight for all overseas consignments provided one can be reasonably certain of a minimum level of demand. This minimum level can be serviced by the cheapest form of freight. Demand above this minimum can be serviced by a faster form of transport. A re-order point is not required for the former unless, and until, the minimum level changes; one way of dealing with the latter is to review the stock balance at a stated period before the next sea shipment is due in. If this is less than the minimum demand for the period plus a pre-determined safety stock, the short-fall is ordered by air. Using the models given in the Appendix, the following summary can be made:

1 *Lead Time—six weeks*	Units
Economic order quantity	350
Average stock level in warehouse	354
Average stock level in transit	528
Minimum safety stock required to avoid stock-out	100

2 *Lead Time—three weeks*	Units
Economic order quantity	350
Average stock level in warehouse	263
Average stock level in transit	273
Minimum safety stock required to avoid stock-out	50

3 *Lead Time*	Units
By sea—6 weeks	
By air—7 days	
Average stock level in warehouse	279
Average stock level in transit	517
Safety stock required to avoid stock-out	10

With regard to the foregoing, the reader should note that this reduction in safety stock can be achieved by sending only 130 units by air throughout the year. In other words, safety stock is reduced by almost as much as it would be if all goods were consigned by air. However, it will be noted that a joint air and sea distribution system of this kind does not have very much effect on the level of in-transit stock and someone is financing this. The models showing the detail of this is given in the appendix.

Whether or not a stock reduction of this magnitude is an economic proposition depends on the value/weight ratio of the product, the cost of holding stock and the additional cost of air freight. In this example average warehouse stock has been reduced by seventy-five units. If this is valued at £1 per unit with a twenty per cent stock-holding cost, the saving is £15. So, provided the additional cost of air is no more than say ten pence per pound, the use of air freight is economic.

From the standpoint of reducing warehouse stock, it is rarely, if ever, necessary to air freight all consignments at a higher cost in order to achieve the maximum economy. On the other hand, a combined air and sea system might very well increase ordering and other documentation costs and these costs, plus the servicing of the in-transit stock, could result in a total air freight movement being cheaper than a combined air and sea system.

The cost comparison given in Figure 5:2 shows how the situation can alter when variables in the equation are changed. Example *A* gives sea freight the advantage; by reducing the rate differential in example *B*, the advantage moves to a combined air and sea system. Double the value of the product, as in example *C*, and an all-air system becomes the cheapest. It should be noted that stock reductions in the market of sale can be justified in certain circumstances to zero. If, for example, the overseas customer will accept a delivery period of up to a week, it may be more economic to have no stock in the country of sale but to supply all orders by air from the factory.

The use of air freight to increase sales involves a straightforward comparison between the incremental profit gained from the additional sales and the additional air cargo rate.

Defining the incremental profit is not quite so straightforward. There is no problem if it is known that the customer will only buy a product if it is delivered by a certain time. If the profit is greater than the extra air cost, then all well and good. Suppose, however, that the air cost is greater than the incremental profit, yet if the particular sale is not made, it might adversely affect the future sales position. It might be a trial order, for example, on the success of which considerable future prospects depend. In these circumstances, it would be a very short-sighted seller who failed to see the value of the investment in air freight.

Unfortunately, not all decisions are so clear cut. Sometimes, a considerable degree of judgement is involved regarding whether or not a particular delivery will have an advantageous, or disadvantageous, effect on the future sales position. One is not always justified in incurring an actual cost now for a hypothetical benefit at a future date.

These problems usually only exist with custom-built products, because standard products can be stocked in the country of sale.

Weight of product	1 lb.			
Product value	£2 per lb			
Density	12 lbs per cu. ft			
Stock-holding costs	20%			
Freight rate: sea	2½p per lb			
air	7½p per lb			
Insurance by sea	25p %			
Insurance by air	20p %			
Interest on money invested	10%			
				£
Average warehouse stock (units):		sea—354	=	708
		air—263	=	526
Average in-transit stock (units):		sea—528	=	1056
		air—273	=	546

10 000 lb consignment	Air cost (£)	Combined air and sea(£)	Sea cost (£)
Cost comparison A			
Consignment value	20 000	20 000	20 000
Freight rate	750	300	250
Stock-holding costs	105	110	142
In-transit stock cost	54	102	106
Documentation	45	70	50
Insurance	40	49	50
	994	631	598
Cost comparison B			
Consignment value	20 000	20 000	20 000
Freight rate	400	260	250
Stock-holdings costs	105	110	142
In-transit stock cost	54	102	106
Documentation	45	70	50
Insurance	40	49	50
	644	591	598
Cost comparison C			
Consignment value	40 000	40 000	40 000
Freight rate	400	260	250
Stock-holding costs	210	220	283
In-transit stock cost	109	205	211
Documentation	45	70	50
Insurance	80	93	100
	844	848	894

FIGURE 5:2 AIR-SEA FREIGHT COMPARATIVE COSTS

6

Depot and plant location

"Nothing astonishes men so much as common sense and plain dealing"
RALPH WALDO EMERSON

Whenever a number of different courses of action are available, some form of calculation must be made to determine which is the best course to take, and the greater the number of different possibilities that exist, the more complicated become the calculations to be made.

To take a simple example, an industrial buyer might want to purchase wire and if he had a complete list of the prices from all sources of supply he could easily determine which was the best buy. But if suppliers offered different levels of quantity discounts, he would have to determine if it were cheaper to buy in larger lots, and store the surplus, or buy in smaller lots at a high unit price. To make this additional calculation, he would need to know the cost of storing the surplus.

If, further, he had the choice of different qualities, all of which could be used in manufacture but each of which had a different effect on the costs of production, the calculations would now be taking on a degree of complexity that might be beyond his capacity to cope with.

Finally, no matter how accurately he made his calculations, they would all be invalidated if a new and hitherto unknown supplier came along with a lower price.

It is problems like these that exist in plant and depot location, i.e.

1 Obtaining complete knowledge about all the possibilities that could exist
2 Making the necessary calculations to find the optimum solution

Distribution as a business activity exists because of the geographical separation between the customer and the point of manufacture. If the customer were willing to collect the goods from where they were made there would be no distribution function. Since the goods have to be delivered to the customer in good condition, the objective must be to do this as cheaply as possible.

Data Collection

If the location of the customer is taken as fixed, there are three variables to consider:

1 Where should the goods be manufactured? This can be further divided into:
  (a) Own manufacture
  (b) Manufacture partly sub-contracted
  (c) Manufacture wholly sub-contracted
2 How should the goods be transported?
  (a) Rail
  (b) Road
  (c) Water
  (d) Air
  (e) Own transport
  (f) Contract transport
3 Where should the goods be stored?
  (a) At point of manufacture
  (b) At point of sale
  (c) At intermediate point

Now it is apparent that there is a tremendous number of possibilities inherent in such a situation. A calculation based on siting a factory in East England may be completely invalidated if it is equally feasible to site the factory in North England.

It is not so readily obvious that it is enormously difficult to collate all the relevant information to permit a calculation of the optimum result. Consider all the cost data that would be required for alternative sitings of a factory—wage rates, rents, utilities, rates, and so on. Consider the practical difficulties involved in getting a complete run-down on all possible competitive freight rates. Add to this the complexity of checking out all possible locations for storage depots and it is clear that, without computers and operational research techniques, it would be a Herculean task to come up with accurate answers.

In order to demonstrate some of the problems and principles involved, it may be appropriate to consider some simple examples.

Example 1
Assume two alternative depot locations and three customers.

	Cost of delivery from Depot (£)	
Customer	A	B
1	1.50	0.75
2	1.00	1.25
3	1.80	3.00
	4.30	5.00

FIGURE 6:1 DELIVERY COSTS (1)

From the data in Figure 6:1, depot *A* is clearly the more economic alternative. However, if the profitability of each customer is concerned, in Figures 6:2 and 6:3, it is seen that the optimum solution is to choose depot *B* and give up customer 3.

Customer	Gross profit (£)	Delivery cost (£) A	Delivery cost (£) B
1	15.00	1.50	0.75
2	18.00	1.00	1.25
3	2.00	1.80	3.00
	35.00	4.30	5.00
	Net profit (£)	30.70	30.00

FIGURE 6:2 DELIVERY COSTS (2)

Customer	Gross profit (£)	Delivery cost (£) A	Delivery cost (£) B
1	15.00	1.50	0.75
2	18.00	1.00	1.25
	33.00	2.50	2.00
	Net Profit (£)	30.50	31.00

FIGURE 6:3 DELIVERY COSTS (3)

On a superficial evaluation of the data, it would still be easy to choose depot *A* because the gross profit of £2, although low, is greater than the delivery cost from depot *A*.

Example 2

Rule-of-thumb calculations can easily lead to wrong conclusions. Figure 6:4 shows the cost per unit of supplying three customers from three different depots.

Customer	Delivery cost from Depot (£) A	Delivery cost from Depot (£) B	Delivery cost from Depot (£) C	Total demand in units
1	0.40	0.55	0.25	100
2	0.30	0.65	0.20	250
3	0.10	0.15	0.40	300
Total supplies available in units	300	270	80	650

FIGURE 6:4 UNIT COSTS

If one were faced with the problem of figuring out the cheapest way to supply all customers it would seem logical to start with the cheapest and then proceed to the next cheapest and so on, as in Figure 6:5.

Depot	Number of units supplied	At price (pence)	To customer	Total (£)
A	300	10	3	30.00
C	80	20	2	16.00
B	170	65	2	110.50
B	100	55	1	55.00
			Total	211.50

FIGURE 6:5 LOWEST COST OF DELIVERY

Once depot *A* had sent its total supply to customer 3, the next cheapest delivery is from depot *C* to customer 2. However, that leaves customer 2 with a short-fall of 170 units which therefore have to be supplied from depot *B*.

But further analysis shows that the important criterion is not the lowest depot-to-customer cost but the lowest average cost from a depot, taking into account the amount it has available and the requirements of all customers.

If the figures are juggled in this way, an alternative solution, as shown by Figure 6:6, would be quite different.

Depot	Number of units supplied	At price (pence)	To customer	Total (£)
A	40	40	1	16.00
A	200	30	2	60.00
A	60	10	3	6.00
B	30	55	1	16.50
B	240	15	3	36.00
C	30	25	1	7.50
C	50	20	2	10.00
			Total	152.00

FIGURE 6:6 LOWEST AVERAGE DELIVERY COST

The total delivery cost here is considerably cheaper, but it is not easy to arrive at these solutions by rule-of-thumb method. One must be careful and not settle for what seems the obvious answer without having a good look at all the other possibilities.

Example 3

Professor P. G. Moore has published an account of how a mechanical model can be set up to illustrate a method of deciding upon the optimum location of a factory to minimise transport costs. A diagram of the model is shown in Figure 6:7.

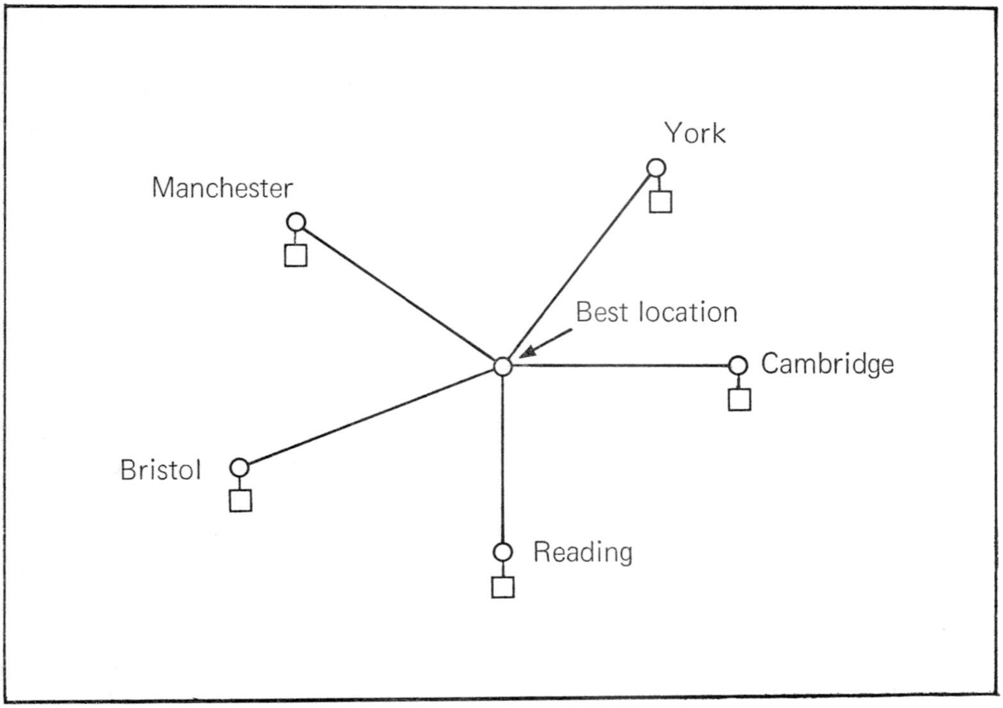

FIGURE 6:7 MODEL OF DEPOT LOCATION

A vertical map shows five different locations, each with a friction-free pulley wheel. Threads are put over each wheel with weights attached to them that are proportional to the demand in each area. If the five threads are joined to the single ring, this ring will settle at a position that represents the optimum location, in terms of transport costs, to serve all five towns.

This model is mathematically correct but, used as a means of finding the optimum location, it fails to take into account any differences that may exist in freight rates between various parts of the country. Another location might, for example, permit the use of freight-liners, or barges, or some other advantageous form of transport, to particular centres.

There are real dangers in setting up over-simplified models because of the risk of over-looking a factor that is important but not obvious. Moreover, nowhere else is the inter-relationship of different functions that is distribution's principal characteristic more apparent than in depot and plant location. Production, warehousing, transport and sales are all involved.

Inter-related Functions

There are two approaches to dealing with the problem and they can best be illustrated by considering the example of a company that has a factory and four depots in the South of England with virtually all its sales in the South. The board of directors decide, as a policy, to expand into the North of England and answers are therefore required to the following questions:

1 What is the forecast of demand for the North classified by product category and geographical area?
2 Can the existing factory service the new market and, if not, can it be expanded; or would it be cheaper to erect another plant in the North or to sub-contract some of the manufacture?
3 Should new depots be established in the North? If so, will it be necessary to review the overall depot situation in the light of the enlarged market and change some of the existing units?

One method of answering questions two and three is to draw up a list of all possible factory locations and all possible depot locations and then to make a separate calculation based on each hypothesis as to what the economic consequences would be. Such calculations would be beyond manual capacity and a computer would have to be used. Input data would have to include all factory costs in each location, all depot costs in each location and all transport costs over every conceivable route. It might also be relevant to assume variations in demand to see what effect this would have on the final result.

In practice, it would almost certainly be preferable to limit the volume of data to be processed by restricting the choice of depot and plant locations and by assuming that transport costs per ton-mile were constant throughout the system. At least this would produce a short list of the more probable locations which could then be checked out in further detail.

The problems involved in data acquisition cannot be over-emphasised. Moreover, there is the expense not only of collecting data, but also of processing it. This has to be taken into account in deciding if the end result is going to be worth the expenditure.

Use of Computer

Since investigations of this kind involve the use of computers it is as well to consider what is involved in terms of the data that have to be fed into the computer and the programming necessary to achieve the desired result.

A company that is setting up a distribution network, served by a number of depots spread over a wide area, needs to know how many depots are required and where they should be sited. It needs to determine an economic location for one or more variable depots in relation to a series of known delivery points and in relation to any depots that may already be in existence. Alternatively, it may need to determine the optimum number of depots required as distinct from finding out the best places to site a given number of depots.

If the only object is to establish that the minimum transport cost and ton-mile cost is standard throughout the area of investigation, then the only variable data to be fed into the computer are the amount to be delivered at each delivery point and any geographical or other barriers to the direct route from a possible location to a delivery point. The calculations required to determine the optimum siting of a fixed number of depots would be quite simple. It would also be fairly straightforward to determine the optimum number of depots required, and no additional data would be needed, provided there was no capacity restriction on a depot. It would only be necessary to increase the number of potential new depots, one at a time, on successive computer runs, determining the minimum ton-mileage for each and then comparing the saving in transport costs with the expense of establishing and maintaining new depots.

Selecting the Best Location for a Depot

One method of doing this would be to superimpose a grid upon a map of the area under consideration. Each square of the grid has a potential depot location as its centre and all individual customers within the square are combined into a single delivery point.

1	2	3	4	5	6
7	8	9	10	11	12
13	14	15	16	17	18
19	20	21	22	23	24
25	26	27	28	29	30
31	32	33	34	35	36

FIGURE 6:8 GRID METHOD OF DEPOT LOCATION

Method

1 Construct a grid of the area with a scale of, say, one inch to one mile over a county or provincial size area and one inch to ten miles over a national area.
2 Estimate total demand arising in each one-inch square and assume that it exists at the centre of the square.

3 Assume a depot location in the centre of each square. If there are known reasons for doing so, eliminate selected squares as possible locations.
4 Calculate the distance from the centre of each square to the centre of all adjoining squares, taking into account any natural obstacles such as rivers that prevent a direct route.
5 For every square that represents a potential location, calculate the ton-miles involved in supplying all demand points from that square.
6 The square involving the lowest number of ton-miles is the optimum site for the depot.

This would be a reasonably accurate method of selecting a single optimum depot site, provided transport costs and depot operating costs were the same throughout the area.

To determine the optimum number of depots in addition to the optimum siting, it would be necessary to continue the analysis to include any combination of two or more squares to determine the number and siting of depots that resulted in the lowest ratio of ton-mileage to depot operating cost.

The square size model depends on the distribution area to be covered and might be anything from one square mile for a county-sized network to ten miles for a national network. All input data for the computer can be recorded with reference to each square and these would have to include any barriers to a direct route and the nearest point at which a barrier could be circumvented.

Computer Programme

The programme for the computer allocates to each depot those delivery points nearest to it after allowing for the circumventing of barriers. Then each depot is moved in relation to its associated delivery points so as to minimise the ton-mileage for that depot. If transport costs vary in different parts of the network, this would have to be taken into account in computing the lowest ton-mile cost for each depot. The forces of the various demands on the depot are then calculated and the depot moved in response to the degree of force until equilibrium is reached.

It will be evident that the demand input data are of critical importance because, unlike the cost and other data used, they involve a degree of uncertainty. The more uncertain demand is, the more important it becomes to cover the range of demand probability in determining where to site depots or plants. If on two extreme demand assumptions, the optimum sitings for a depot are Warwick and Northampton, the law of probability might prudently suggest some intermediate point.

Lastly, one must never overlook the human factor. A programmed computer will precisely calculate recorded cost data but it will not be able to take into account such factors as the availability of labour, the willingness of staff to move house, the effect of environment on morale and productivity. But this management must do if computer calculations and operational research techniques are to have any real validity.

Future Changes

Once established, a factory or warehouse is expected to be in service for a long time. It is important, therefore, that when the optimum number or the optimum siting of locations is being determined, sufficient account is taken of any likely future changes that could alter the economic balance. One factor that has already been mentioned is a change in demand. If one market area rises or falls in relation to another, this could well affect plans for optimum siting. But changes in costs could be equally relevant. Wage rates in a rapidly developing area, for example, might be expected to rise faster than elsewhere. Transport developments could reasonably be expected to alter the cost balance between one site and another.

If the geographical area under consideration spanned more than one country it would become appropriate to consider such factors as anticipated changes in tax policies or the degree of currency inflation that might exist between one country and another.

7

The cost of lost sales

"*All great truths begin as blasphemies*"
George Bernard Shaw

The cost of lost sales is one of the most neglected areas of business study. This may be partly due to the fact that to examine the cost of lost sales involves an admission that sales have been lost, and this is something that sales departments are understandably reluctant to concede unless it is demonstrable that the loss is the fault of some other department. But it is undoubtedly also due to the difficulties that arise in trying to measure the cost of the lost sales.

It is important to avoid any confusion between the causes of lost sales and their cost. Orders can be lost for all sorts of reasons—price, product quality, delivery and so on—and a distinction must be made between those reasons that are directly measurable and those that are infinitely variable in measurement. Price is a good example. Almost any price can be said to lose some sales for a product if a price reduction will increase demand. The optimum price is that which yields the largest profit. The same characteristics apply to product quality to which can be allied such attributes as "built-in obsolescence", safety and convenience. A company will tend to have a product cost structure that will produce the highest profit within the limits set by market price.

The cost with which the distribution function has to concern itself is the cost of failing to deliver, or to have available, a product that is in demand at an economic price. This failure can be due to two causes:

1 Wrong sales forecast
2 Failure to have stock available to meet a demand that has been accurately forecast (this can be a manufacturing failure or a stock control failure)

The first point to establish is that failure to deliver actually results in a lost sale, and here it is necessary to distinguish between custom-built goods and standard goods because only the latter can be stocked.

Custom-built Goods

Custom-built goods are ordered to a customer's specification; this may be for a bespoke tailored suit, a cake-wrapping machine or printed notepaper. If the goods are delivered late, or not at all, will this prejudice future sales? If future sales are not affected, then no damage has been done; but this is something that it is extremely difficult to be sure about and it calls for objective judgement from the company selling the goods.

There is some evidence that, in many industries, a convention on delivery exists, which, while unintelligible to overseas customers, is implicitly accepted within the country by all the parties to a contract. A buyer requires a machine in, say, September. The seller quotes three-months delivery, but the buyer knows from experience it is going to be six weeks late so he orders it for July. The seller knows that the buyer knows that he is going to be six weeks late so, when he finally delivers in September, everyone is happy. In such an environment the seller is justified in assuming that late delivery is not costing him sales, although he might be well advised to consider if a different environment exists in his overseas markets.

Another factor to consider is whether a cure of the cause of the late delivery will involve a cost. If no cost is involved, then a cure might be recommended on grounds of business sensibility. But if, to cure the fault costs money, because for example, it would involve employing a production engineer or using a computer bureau, then it must be established that the cure will result in additional sales in the long run where the incremental profit exceeds the cost of the cure.

Standard Goods

Standard goods can be stocked but this is not to say that market convention requires that they be readily available from stock. Fast-moving consumer goods like food, drink, cigarettes and so on must be immediately available. But for many items of furniture, for typewriters, pianos, office desks and so on, there is a delivery period that becomes acceptable for each item. One would accept a delivery of, say, three months for a computer but would expect an adding maching to be delivered in a week or two.

A failure to supply standard goods is in the first place a failure of stock. The stock may not be available for many reasons but it is because the stock is not there that the sale is lost. Analysis must therefore focus on two questions:

1 How much business is lost because of the failure to supply?
2 What is the cost of removing the cause of the failure to supply?

In answering the first question, the problem hinges on whether a failure to supply results in a loss of the single sale under consideration and whether it will prejudice future sales as well. This depends partly on whether the product is in recurrent, or non-recurrent, demand. An example is cigarettes; the customer may purchase daily and a failure to supply might, in addition to losing that particular sale, have two further adverse consequences. It could lose future business because the customer decides to shop elsewhere; the customer might also influence other customers to take their business away. A simple illustration will demonstrate this. A surburban businessman buys twenty *brand x* cigarettes at a certain shop *en route* to the station each morning. The customer is invariably accompanied by two colleagues who also buy twenty cigarettes daily of a different brand. One day the customer finds the shop is out of stock of *brand x*. This happens three days in one week and so the customer not only starts buying from another shop but induces his colleagues to do so as well. Assuming twopence profit for twenty cigarettes and assuming further that all three would have otherwise continued to purchase from the shop for another 100 weeks, the profit loss to the shopkeeper (five days a week) is:

$$2p \times 5 \text{ (days)} \times 100 \text{ (weeks)} \times 3 \text{ (customers)} = £30.$$

Clearly, had the shopkeeper been aware of all these facts, he would have been justified in keeping much larger stocks of *brand x* merely to satisfy that one customer.

In considering a product in non-recurrent demand, say an encyclopaedia or a piano—the seller has to judge if a failure to satisfy a demand from a single customer is going to affect adversely potential sales either because:

(a) the unsatisfied customer induces other would-be buyers not to buy or
(b) the unsatisfied customer decides as a consequence not to buy some other product from the same seller or
(c) the seller gains a wider reputation for bad delivery, which adversely affects his sales.

The door-to-door salesman selling vacuum cleaners does not do as much harm to himself through losing a sale because of delivery as does a piano dealer who might also hope to sell the same customer sheet music or gramophone records.

Whilst it is not too difficult to state the problem, to suggest a solution calls for careful thought, distinguishing throughout between the consumer market and the industrial market.

Consumer Market

In the consumer market, goods are usually sold through retail outlets and so, looking at the problem from the retailer's standpoint to begin with, it is easy to see that he can best minimise the risk of lost sales by ensuring that a record is kept of every demand from customers for products that are not in stock. The one-man business tends to do this automatically because, when re-ordering, he is aware of what customers have been asking for. In a larger retail outlet, it would become necessary to set up a formal re-ordering system with each member of the sales staff required to note any lost sales because the item was not in stock. This would not only serve as a check on the effectiveness of stock control on existing lines; it would also indicate when new lines should be stocked.

The wholesaler is in much the same position. Since a multiplicity of lines are handled, accurate information is required on whether sales are lost, either because of ineffective stock control or because of a failure of supply on the part of the manufacturer. Again, all that is required is a simple system for recording unfulfilled demand and then taking the appropriate corrective action.

The manufacturer of consumer goods is in a somewhat different position, because whilst he must be in a position to supply demand from wholesalers and retailers, he also frequently has to accept responsibility for creating or increasing the consumer demand that is channelled through wholesalers and retailers. A manufacturer of dog-leads will concentrate on getting retail outlets to stock and display his products. A manufacturer of dog food will have to promote his product in order to stimulate the demand laid on the retailers and, in this instance, it is often difficult to assess what demand will arise from any given promotion.

In the consumer market, it can be safely assumed that it is always dangerous to lose sales of products in recurrent demand and the greater the brand consciousness associated with the product, the bigger the danger is. However, avoiding such lost sales is not difficult, given effective stock control throughout the chain of distribution from manufacturer to retail sale, provided, of course, that the level of sales has been accurately forecast.

Industrial Market

In the industrial market, on the other hand, different problems arise which make the task of measuring lost sales more complex. If a customer is assumed to make a demand that cannot be fulfilled because it is not in stock, or cannot be made available at the time it is wanted, the possible consequences can be as set out in Figure 7:1.

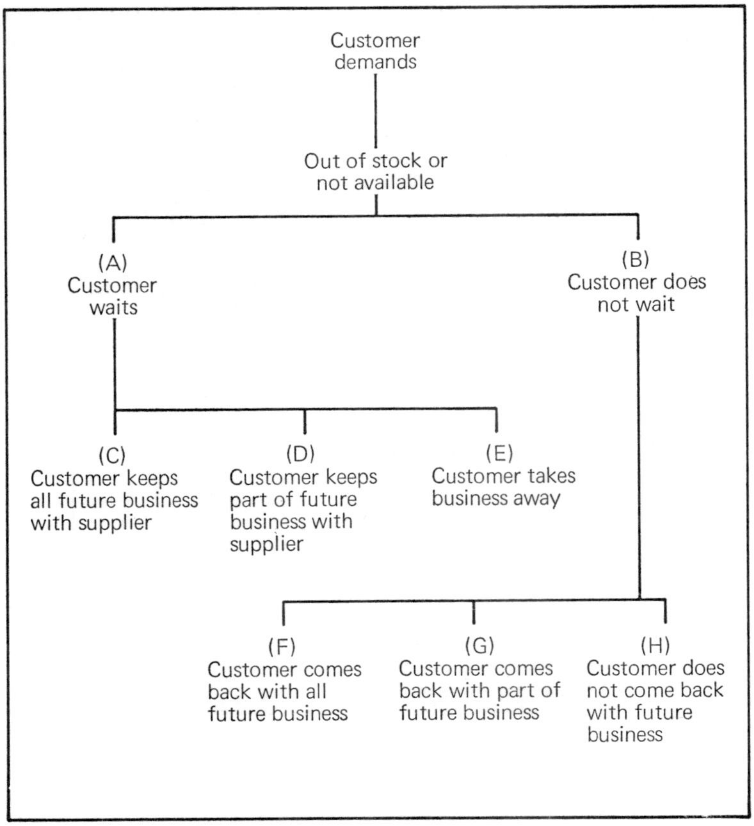

FIGURE 7:1 DIAGRAM OF SUPPLY FAILURE

The consequences to the supplier of failing to supply when demanded can be:

AC, AD, AE, BF, BG, BH

With AC, nothing is lost. But with BH, everything is lost. Which of the other consequences is best for the supplier depends on the profit in the initial demand and the likelihood of demand recurring. If a company were supplied with an inter-communication system, consequence AE might be preferred to consequence BF. If selling office stationery, on the other hand, with all the potential for repeat business, BF is preferred to AE.

What a supplier of industrial goods must do, therefore, is, on the one hand, to measure the cost of fulfilling a demand and, on the other, to measure the cost of failing to fulfil it. The first cost is readily determined by conventional accounting procedures and is a combination of manufacturing, storage and transport expenses. The second cost is not conventionally recorded and some innovation must take place if it is to be measured. There are two estimates to be made:

1 The profit loss from the existing order
2 The profit loss from all future orders

The ability to measure profit loss from existing orders depends on the circumstances. If a customer threatens to cancel an order for a machine unless delivery is obtained by a given date, the profit on the order can be compared to the cost of achieving such delivery. A supplier of adding machines, on the other hand, cannot be sure that a stock-out, at any particular time, will lose a given number of orders.

It is possible, however, to assign a factor to every existing and potential customer which would make some estimate feasible and a simple illustration (see Figure 7:2) gives some indication of what can be done.

Assume the analysis for a company's customers in one year as in Figure 7:2.

Number of customers	Order value (£) × 1000	Turnover (£)	Per cent profit	Profit (£)	Profit per customer (£)
2	Over 50	140 000	5	7 000	3500
8	25–50	250 000	6	15 000	1875
18	20–25	396 000	8	31 680	1750
34	15–20	578 000	10	57 800	1700
126	10–15	1 512 000	10	151 200	1200
40	Under 10	320 000	10	32 000	800

FIGURE 7:2 CUSTOMER VALUE ANALYSIS

Looking at these facts in isolation, one would readily deduce that it is worth spending quite a bit to retain the custom of the top two customers with the remainder being considered in relation to their profit contribution, ranging from £1875 to £800.

If, however, the analysis is continued to include the probability of their remaining customers over the next five years, the results in Figure 7:3 might emerge.

Number of customers	Order value (£) × 1000	Probability of existing level of business continuing over 5 years (%)	This year's profit (£)	Next 5 years' profit (£)	Total profit (£)	Total profit per customer (£)
	Over 50					
2		5	7 000	1 750	8 750	4375
	25–50					
4		50	7 500	18 750	26 250	6560
2		20	3 750	3 750	7 500	3750
2		10	3 750	1 875	5 625	2812
	20–25					
6		60	10 500	31 500	42 000	7000
4		50	7 000	17 500	24 500	6125
2		40	3 500	7 000	10 500	5250
6		30	10 500	15 750	26 250	4375
	15–20					
8		80	13 600	54 400	68 000	8500
10		70	17 000	59 500	76 500	7650
2		60	3 400	10 200	13 600	6800
6		40	10 200	20 400	30 600	5100
8		20	13 600	13 600	27 200	3400
	10–15					
20		90	24 000	108 000	132 000	6600
16		80	19 200	76 800	96 000	6000
30		70	36 000	126 000	162 000	5400
26		50	31 200	78 000	109 200	4200
14		30	16 800	25 200	42 000	3000
20		10	24 000	12 000	36 000	1800
	Under 10					
20		90	16 000	72 000	88 000	4400
20		80	6 000	64 000	80 000	4000

FIGURE 7:3 CUSTOMER PROBABILITY ANALYSIS

The analysis shows that, far from the top two customers (in total profit contribution) being the most important to look after for the future, pride of place is held by customers in the £15 000-to-£20 000 turnover range.

This is, of course, a contrived example and it might be argued that it is fanciful to try to measure the probability of a customer remaining a customer for the next five years. But the act of trying to measure the probability often produces enlightening results. Previous experience may show that larger customers are more prone to be fickle than small customers. The advent of new competition may be more likely to wean one category of customer away than another.

Who is to assign these probabilities? It should not be left exclusively to salesmen who may be, by training and temperament, unsuited to making objective assessments about a customer's future buying intentions. Certainly the salesman must contribute to the judgement, but it should be reviewed by an authority on the marketing or financial side of the business.

How to Apportion Selling Costs in a Multi-product Sales Operation

The objective here is simply to apportion each category of selling expense to each product line so as to determine when the cost of selling any particular product line is becoming too high.

Selling costs	Product *A*	Product *B*	Product *C*	Total (£)
Sales management	3 000	2 000	2 000	7 000
Marketing/Market Research	3 000	1 000	1 000	5 000
Field selling	12 000	15 000	8 000	35 000
Sales office	4 000	4 000	4 000	12 000
Exhibitions/leaflets etc.	—	1 000	2 000	3 000
Advertising	—	—	2 000	2 000
Total	22 000	23 000	19 000	64 000
Annual sales	150 000	190 000	80 000	420 000
Selling cost as percentage of sales	14.6	12.1	23.8	15.2

FIGURE 7:4 EXAMPLE OF SELLING EXPENSE APPORTIONED TO PRODUCT

In Figure 7:4 scrutiny of total costs alone would tend to conceal the high cost of selling product *C*.

Following the example given in Figure 7:4 two forms are included in this chapter which the reader may be able to use in a practical way. These can be either simply copied or expanded to suit the reader's particular requirements. Figure 7:5 corresponds to Figure 7:4 and Figure 7:6 can be used to analyse lost sales.

SELLING COSTS	Product *A*			Product *B*			Product *C*			Total		
	This mth	Last mth	Prev. mth	This mth	Last mth	Prev. mth	This mth	Last mth	Prev. mth	This mth	Last mth	Prev. mth
Sales management Sales office Field selling Commissions Royalties Advertising Promotions Exhibitions Miscellaneous												
Total												
Sales												
Selling costs as percentage of sales												

FIGURE 7:5 SELLING COSTS

Lost Sales

Lost sales are defined as the value and nature of demands that it was not possible to fulfil.

Product	Demand this month	Demand last month	Demand in previous month
1			
2			
3			
4			
5			
6			

FIGURE 7:6 LOST SALES

8

Component supply in distribution

"A man should never be ashamed to own he has been in the wrong, which is but saying, in other words, that he is wiser today than he was yesterday"
JONATHAN SWIFT

A central maxim of modern distribution practice is the importance of looking at the total distribution cost picture rather than at individual cost elements. By examining all the variables in the equation, it is possible to exploit all opportunities for trade-off economics and thus achieve the lowest possible total cost of distribution.

With good organisation, any firm can do this successfully in so far as its own operation is concerned, because it controls all the functions that create the cost of distribution.

In a situation where a number of different and autonomous companies are contributing towards a finished product, a further set of problems arise which will now be examined in detail.

The problems arise, of course, because the individual companies are autonomous and there is, therefore, no single person or organisation with the information and authority to enable the optimum method of distribution to be achieved.

The parameters of the problem can be seen by considering a simple example involving four different companies contributing towards the manufacture of a machine consisting of a casting, machined parts and electrical components:

Company
A supplies the casting
B machines the parts
C manufactures the electrical components
D assembles, tests and sells the machine

If it is an entirely custom-built machine with no standard parts, the time and cost elements in the operation depend on how long it takes each company to carry out its function. If all the work is special to that machine, no stocks are involved and the customer will have to wait the full manufacturing cycle. Price, moreover, will not be very significant, because competition is not so readily available.

If it is a standard machine, the amount and quality of competition becomes significant in terms of the delivery period that is acceptable and the price that can be charged.

The price build-up of the finished product can be set out as follows:

	Company
A	manufacturing cost
	storage cost
	transport cost
	profit
B	machining cost
	storage cost
	transport cost
	profit
C	manufacturing and assembly cost
	storage cost
	transport cost
	profit
D	assembly cost
	storage cost
	profit
Total =	price of machine

It is apparent that, if any or all of these costs can be reduced, there is an overall margin available either to decrease the price or increase the total profit. If one organisation or individual controlled all these functions, it would be possible to set up a procedure for ensuring that all the various activities were dovetailed in the most economic manner. And the lynch-pin of the whole operation would be the forecast of how many machines it was going to be possible to sell.

Autonomous Companies

In practice, because each company is autonomous, each sets up machinery to protect what it considers to be its own interest and the cumulative effect is to increase the total cost of supply.

Company *D* are the main contractors. They sell the machine to the customer and are responsible for delivery. They also forecast sales. Their defence mechanism, in dealing with their sub-contractors, is firstly, to tend to exaggerate the amount they expect to sell and secondly, to tend to ask for their supplies before they really need them. They do this so as to try to ensure that their sub-contractors are going to be able to supply all their components on the most optimistic assumptions of what will be sold.

The principal problem of the sub-contractors is estimating what the main contractor is going to require. They are restricted by lead times on the supply of raw materials, and so on. If the main contractor's forecast is too optimistic and he subsequently cuts back, the sub-contractor may find himself over-stocked. In practice, the sub-contractor either learns from experience, or suspects that the main contractor will be forecasting over-optimistically, and so he tends to revise the estimates downwards on the basis of what, by the nature of things, can be no more than a "hunch". This means that if sales are as high as the main contractor suggested, he fails to supply all that is required and delivery to the final customer suffers. If the main contractor has alternative suppliers for the same components, this may create further insecurity among the sub-contractors, who are forced to make judgements based on inadequate information.

Looking at the total supply picture the following unfavourable economic consequences can ensue:

1 The machines are late on delivery because components are not ready for assembly
2 Sub-contractors' stocks rise with a danger of deterioration or obsolescence
3 Transport costs rise because of the necessity to "rush" components in short supply or to speed up a machine delivery that is already late
4 Assembly costs rise because of component shortage
5 Main contractor component stocks rise because of the need for a further "buffer" to protect against supply uncertainty.

Some uncertainty is, of course, inherent in the situation because no one can be sure what the customer will want and when. But it is clear that the difficulties are being aggravated because each company is taking separate action designed to protect its own interests. Because of a lack of free and open communication, the total cost of supply becomes more expensive than it need be. The main contractor frequently overlooks the fact that if sub-contractors can be persuaded to carry higher stocks than are really necessary, action is being taken that inevitably increases the cost of the machine being sold.

This simple example reveals the basic problems of component supply. But there is an even more serious difficulty that crops up in large-scale operations and this is the time-lag.

Time-Lag Problems

To explain the nature of the problem, the example is taken of component supply to a heavy commercial vehicle manufacturer. A vehicle manufacturer makes surprisingly little of the vehicles it supplies and in many cases none at all. The various parts, such as engines, clutches, shock absorbers, brakes, are provided by a multitude of component suppliers whilst the vehicle firms, in the main, confine themselves to designing, assembling and selling the finished product. In the heavy commercial vehicle market, the problem is more pronounced because there is a good deal less standardisation than there is with motor cars. A heavy commercial vehicle assembly line invariably comprises units that are designated for particular customers, most of whom will have at least some special requirements.

The time-lag problem can best be seen by examining the sequence of events that takes place in the supply of components.

The first step is that the vehicle builder resolves the quantities of each model required for manufacture in the ensuing period. This build programme, which is based on a forecast of what the manufacturer's sales department expects to sell, might look like the hypothetical example set out in Figure 8:1.

A.B.C. Truck Manufacturing Co. Ltd.
Build Programme July to Sept

Model	Wheels	GVW	Forecast
BW	4	12	60
CN	4	12	25
CNN	6	16	110
FJ	6	18	20
CT	8	22	90
ABB	8	24	50
			355

FIGURE 8:1 BUILD PROGRAMME

The build programme is given to the manufacturer's materials department with instructions to order the necessary components. On the assumption that the build programme refers only to current models, for which the suppliers are established, the materials staff then place orders with suppliers using a schedule which stipulates a certain weekly or monthly call-off for, say, the following three months (see Figure 8:2). These schedules will normally take into account existing stocks and in particular the buffer stock which will tend to be proportionately higher for those models with a smaller and more irregular demand.

A.B.C. Truck Manufacturing Co. Ltd.

Material schedule	To Supplier XYZ Axle Co. Ltd.		
Axle type	Month 1	Month 2	Month 3
01	25	25	25
02	40	40	40
03	20	30	30
04	40	60	60

FIGURE 8:2 MATERIAL SCHEDULE

When the schedules reach the component supplier, the latter will invariably have to translate them on to his own internal documentation, because each customer will be sending material schedules in a different form and this will require standardisation. This is inevitably a laborious and time-consuming manual process.

When all the customers' material schedules have been standardised internally, the next step is for the supplier to provision the material necessary to meet the demand. The demand is then resolved, in terms of assemblies, into the component parts of these assemblies. This is done because account has to be taken of the commonalty of component parts between different assemblies. There may be thousands of these individual components to provision and if commonalty exists, the easier, and cheaper, the task becomes.

None the less, it is a formidable undertaking because the stock controller responsible for this operation has to keep some form of record—perhaps a stock card—which lists the current stock of the part, the procurement re-order time and the usage. Account must be taken of the fact that the part can either be completely bought-in, partly bought-in and worked on in the factory or, fully machined and manufactured from raw material in the factory.

Periodically, stock cards for demand and procurement lead time must be updated, otherwise surplus stock or shortage situations will ensue.

Economics of Component Assembly

The assembly of the components presents no problem provided all the individual parts are there to be assembled. In these circumstances, finished assembly stocks are a function of assembly shop economics. The prime point to remember, however, is that if the customer's demand for assemblies is continuously changing, as in practice it often is, the supplier can only satisfy this demand if he has in stock, ready to be assembled, all the parts required for the components in demand. Since the notice given by the customer, stated on his material schedules, is often very short—and certainly much shorter than the total manufacturing lead time—this point becomes of paramount importance. The individual parts of components must be manufactured before the demand for them arises and this means manufacturing on a forecast of sale.

Forecasting sales in these circumstances is extremely speculative. If this is done by looking at historical data, there are many areas of uncertainty to falsify the trend, such as:

1 Stock adjustments by truck manufacturer
2 Changes in the sales pattern of individual vehicle models
3 The extent to which demand can change, from the ultimate buyer of a truck, for those parts that are optional (those not common to every vehicle)

However, if adequate information can be obtained about the manufacturer's stock situation, this would be a reasonably accurate method of forecasting. The problem of the time-lag lies in the time involved for each stage in the process such as:

Time taken by manufacturer to prepare and issue material schedules	.... say, three weeks

Time taken by supplier to transfer customer's schedule on to internal documentation and passing to stock controller .... say, three weeks

Time taken between each up-dating of parts stock card .... say, six weeks

This means that if demand for a particular truck starts to rise at, say, the beginning of June, it is the beginning of September before the supplier is effectively taking steps to meet that demand by increasing the usage on the parts stock card. The supplier, therefore, fails to meet the rising demand on time. The more demand goes on rising, the more the difficulties are compounded.

If, conversely, demand starts falling, the time needed for corrective action to be taken results in overstocking with the attendant dangers of stock deterioration or obsolescence.

Why not up-date the stock cards more frequently—this will at least reduce the major cause of delay? The problem here is the magnitude of the task. A manual task of up-dating of tens of thousands of cards cannot very well be done every week and, indeed, experience shows that even if it is planned to up-date every six weeks, it is only too easy for this time to become longer for some, if not the majority, of the cards, because of the difficulties of control and supervision. Computer up-dating is a complex and certainly a very expensive operation due to the number of changes that have to be made to the input data.

It is clear that all these difficulties could be overcome if the time-lag were eliminated. Trying to reduce the time involved in each process by the use of better methods would provide a partial solution but, again, it would be difficult and costly to control.

Provisioning on "Mean" Forecasts

One solution, that does effectively eliminate the time-lag, is to provision the parts, not from customers' schedules but direct from the actual build of vehicles.

The supplier can set up a schedule of assemblies used on each truck model and, if the truck manufacturer is able to provide the information, the supplier can establish an average weekly forecast of sale for each truck. This will automatically determine the number of standard components required. For optional parts, an average usage figure can be agreed with the truck manufacturer. If the manufacturer also gives details of the stock held, the supplier can automatically allow for this when provisioning.

The truck manufacturer must then furnish the supplier with a daily or weekly record of the trucks that are built—a simple enough matter that can be done by telephone. If the actuals are moving to either side of the average, an immediate adjustment is made by the component supplier stock controller.

This now becomes a much more manageable operation for data processing. The computer can be programmed on average figures and the only input changes that have to be made each week are on a truck model basis and not on the basis of the individual parts.

Such a system would not affect the manufacturer's material schedules. These would still be issued and fulfilled from the supplier's finished assembly warehouse. Because the provisioning of the parts is now directly geared to the trucks being built, the risk of under- or over-supply of parts is greatly diminished and the truck manufacturer gets a much better service.

Although such a solution would provide more efficiency, the reduction in distribution costs is not always obvious because it is shared between the manufacturer and supplier. Moreover, there is an inevitable reluctance on the part of the manufacturer to release sales and build-schedule information to suppliers. This can sometimes be reinforced by the motivation of the manufacturer's materials department who might sometimes feel that such a close distribution liaison with their supplier would reduce their authority and perhaps diminish their significance.

Distribution starts with production planning and ends with delivery to the customer. Unless all the processes involved are viewed together, the cost of distribution may not be kept to a minimum.

Two Solutions

There are two ultimate solutions to the problem of component supply. One is for the main contractor and sub-contractors to get together to find the best answer. To do this, there must be a completely free exchange of information and some surrender of independence by individual suppliers. It is not easy for companies to do this, but at least the main contractors should be open about the degree of uncertainty involved in their forecasts. Concerted efforts (perhaps a committee of supply with representatives from each major sub-contractor would be established) would tend to diminish the unfavourable consequence of the time-lag.

The second way is to have commonalty of parts. If five different models of truck can be produced from only two different kinds of engines, axles, gearboxes and so on, then the difficulties of supply are minimised and this of course is what all manufacturers seek to do.

If, however, the manufacturer and the component supplier are considered together, this economic advantage can be developed further. If a gearbox manufacturer can provide a whole range of gearboxes from the same component parts, then so far as machining activity is concerned, it does not matter what product is required, it can be done on a minimum safety stock level. It is only when specific parts are prepared for particular models that substantial safety stocks must be held, if a highly irregular demand is to be satisfied. Moreover, it is easier for the manufacturer to obtain adequate supplies of bought-out components without the need for large safety stocks.

So far as assembly is concerned, the situation depends on whether or not all or most of the fitters are capable of assembling all the gearbox models. If they are, the sales mix is not economically significant from the standpoint of the procurement of the parts.

If it is assumed that all the component parts are available for any foreseeable demand, then the average stock level in the supplier's finished assembly warehouse will depend on how long the assembly process takes and how the frequency distribution of demand appears. This concerns the likelihood of a particular level of demand arising at irregular and infrequent intervals but which is so essential that it has to be satisfied. The only way to be almost 100 per cent sure of satisfying such an irregular demand is to carry a very large safety stock of the assembly in question. There can be no doubt that the only way to keep down safety stock levels, in the finished goods warehouse, is to keep assembly time as short as possible.

Commonalty of Parts

Considering the stock of component parts, the situation can be quite different according to the commonalty of parts that exist in the finished product mix. If a component part is specific to an assembly then its stock level will be determined in exactly the same way as that of the assembly, except that the supply lead time, instead of comprising only assembly time, consists also of the time taken to buy in and/or, machine the parts. The same supply lead time also applies to common parts but the paramount distinction between the specific and common parts lies in the amount of safety stock necessary to satisfy any given frequency distribution of demand.

For example, let it be assumed that there are three specific parts, the average demand for each of which is 100 units per week but whose demand characteristics are such that demand can rise as high as 150 in any week. This is the demand that must be catered for. Safety stock necessary to cover this probability is, say, twenty-five units for each part, making a total safety stock of seventy-five units.

It will be noted that the total safety stock is designed to cover the probability that demand for all three specific parts could peak to 150 units *in the same week or in three separate weeks.*

If the three specific parts are replaced by a single common part then the probability of average weekly demand rising from 300 units to a peak of 450 units in the same week is demonstrably more remote than the probability of three separate demands, each averaging 100 units a week, each peaking to 150 units in any week. Therefore, the safety stock requirement to cover the same level of demand would drop from seventy-five to say thirty-five units by the substitution of a common part. This is probably the most important factor affecting the economics of component supply.

Determination of the Economic Manufacturing Batch Quantity

(a)	(b)	(c)	(d)	(e)	(f)	(g)
Number of units produced in batch	Cost per unit	Number of units produced annually	Annual manufacturing cost	Average stock level	Annual stock-holding cost	Total annual cost

FIGURE 8:3 MANUFACTURING AND STOCK-HOLDING COSTS

The use of Figure 8:3 will determine the most economic balance between unit manufacturing cost in batch production and stock-holding cost, where the unit cost of manufacturing varies according to the size of the batch.

1 Columns (a) to (d) inclusive, in Figure 8:3, summarise the different costs of production according to the size of the manufacturing batch.
2 The stock-holding cost, columns (e) to (f), is a function of the average amount of stock in the warehouse and the percentage cost of holding cost, which is calculated in accordance with the guide given in Chapter 4, Figure 4:10. If, for example, the average quantity of production in stock has a value of £100 000 and the percentage cost of holding stock is twenty per cent, then the figure that goes in column (f) is £20 000.
3 Add columns (d) and (f) to give total annual cost in column (g). The lowest total in column (g) will correspond with the most economic batch quantity in column (a).

9

Overseas distribution

"The old order changeth, yielding place to new, and God fulfils himself in many ways, lest one good custom should corrupt the World."

TENNYSON

There is no fundamental economic distinction between national distribution and international distribution—the same problems apply to both and the same solutions are available. The reasons why overseas distribution merits separate study are twofold:

1 Communication is nearly always more difficult internationally, because of language and distance
2 In most situations, the exporter does not control the overseas selling and distribution organisation

In Chapter 10 it is stated that optimum distribution efficiency cannot be achieved unless one executive in a business has the knowledge and authority to be able to evaluate and seize the opportunities that exist for trade-off economies between production, transport, storage and sale. If this is a valid statement, it applies as much overseas as it does on the domestic market. It will be apparent that it is not only difficult to evaluate the situation internationally, because of the absence of adequate information, it is even more difficult to enforce a solution on an autonomous and foreign organisation.

In this chapter, two examples are given of how the efficiency of international distribution can be increased if the problems of communication can be overcome. One example deals with the export of a standard product, which has to be stocked. The other is concerned with custom-built products and shows that distribution is not entirely a function of transportation and storage.

It must be said quite plainly that there is no hope of achieving optimum distribution unless the overseas selling organisation is considered as part of the home selling organisation. The fatal mistake is to regard the overseas selling organisation as a customer from whom orders are received.

Minimising Overseas Stocks

To illustrate the first example, it is assumed that a British manufacturer is marketing a range of products in six overseas countries, where his agents have the following annual sales:

Country	Sales (£)
A	100 000
B	150 000
C	80 000
D	240 000
E	30 000
F	120 000
Total	720 000

The value/weight ratio of all products is £4 per kilogramme and it takes the manufacturer an average of six weeks to process the orders he receives from his overseas agents. Because each agent's lead time is six weeks plus transit time, which varies according to the destination, each is required by the manufacturer to carry three months' stock. Because the manufacturer is realistic, he gives each agent three months' credit to ensure that this is done. This money tied up in overseas stocks is worth twenty per cent to him and is therefore costing £36 000 a year. The surface transit time taken to deliver the goods to each country is as follows:

Country	Transit Time (days)
A	12
B	20
C	16
D	12
E	14
F	8

The reason each agent carries three months' stock—to provide the ninety-nine per cent in-stock reliability that the manufacturer requires—is because it takes him six weeks, plus transit time, to get his orders filled. To reduce these overseas stocks, the lead time must be shortened, but it does not provide a solution merely to reduce transit time by using air transport instead of sea transport. If transit time by sea is twelve days and by air one day, then shifting to air only reduces total lead time from just under eight weeks to just over six weeks, and this will not permit much reduction in overseas stocks.

If, however, the manufacturer can reduce order processing time to two days—which he can only do by holding stocks himself—then it can make sense to use air freight, because total lead time can then be reduced to three days. It must be emphasised that, from the agent's point of view, he must be able to feel certain about a three-day lead time; his chief enemy is uncertainty.

If the agent can be certain of a three-day lead time, it is safe to assume that he can operate on a one-week inventory.

The manufacturer, who has to process orders in two days, must always keep a stock and it is unlikely that the total stock level necessary to satisfy the aggregate of demand from all six areas would exceed three weeks' sale. Therefore, the total stock in the system can be reduced from three months to one month. The actual stock level that would be required depends on the frequency distribution of demand and the degree of in-stock reliability it was desired to maintain but, for any given frequency distribution of demand, there must be a correlation between necessary stock levels in the overseas market and at the point of manufacture.

Taking into account the additional cost of air freight to each market, the overall transportation charge on a complete conversion to air freight can be calculated and compared with the reduction in stock-holding cost that this achieves.

Country	Annual sales (£)	Weight of annual shipments in kilos	Additional cost of air freight per kilo (pence)	Additional cost of air freight per year (£)
A	100 000	25 000	5	1 250
B	150 000	37 500	8	3 000
C	80 000	20 000	7	1 400
D	240 000	60 000	5	3 000
E	30 000	7 500	6	450
F	120 000	30 000	4	1 200
				10 300
Four weeks' stock-holding cost by manufacturer and overseas agents				11 060
				22 360
			Net savings	13 640

FIGURE 9:1 FREIGHT COSTS

However, further examination reveals that this may not be the optimum solution. If the manufacturer stocks at the point of manufacture, lead times are reduced to sea transit time plus two days for order processing. This in itself will permit some reduction in stock levels, without any use of air freight at all and this may conservatively be assumed as shown in Figure 9:2.

If sea transport is used exclusively, necessary stock levels in each country would tend to be relatively higher because, for example, the probability of a three-day delay by surface transport would be greater than the probability of a one-day delay by air transport. There is a greater element of uncertainty involved and this will apply an upward pressure to overseas stocks. For these reasons, it is unlikely that net savings would be as high as £13 940.

Nevertheless, it is theoretically possible that, even without the use of air freight, a quite substantial reduction in stock throughout the system could be achieved although the saving would not be as great as with a total use of air.

Country	Transit time by sea (days)	Overseas minimum stock levels (weeks)	Stock-holding costs at 20% (£)
A	12	4	1 600
B	20	8	4 630
C	16	6	1 850
D	12	4	3 700
E	14	5	580
F	8	3	1 380

At point of manufacture: Three weeks' stock	£ 8 320
Total stock costs	£22 060
Total savings	£13 940

FIGURE 9:2 STOCK LEVEL REDUCTION COSTS

However, since the relationship between necessary stock levels and the additional cost of air transport varies from one country to another, analysis reveals that the optimum solution lies in using air freight to countries B, C and E and surface transport to countries A, D and F. The result can be seen summarised in Figure 9:3.

Country	Stock held (weeks)	Stock-holding costs (£)	Additional cost of air freight (£)
A	4	1 600	—
B	1	580	3 000
C	1	308	1 400
D	4	3 700	—
E	1	115	450
F	3	1 380	—
Manufacturer		8 320	—
		16 003	4 850

Total	£20 853
Net saving maximised at	£15 147

FIGURE 9:3 OPTIMUM SOLUTION

Further analysis might show even greater scope for savings by a combined use of air and sea shipments to each country but enough has been said to show that the way to achieve the greatest benefit is to consider both ends of international distribution as part of the same operation. There are several variables in the equation as the following summary shows:

1 *Overseas stock levels* The higher these are the more opportunity exists for reducing the aggregate level in the system by stocking at the point of manufacture and reducing the order processing time to a minimum.

2 *Value of Product* The lower the value/weight ratio of the product the higher will be the cost of air freight as a percentage of value, since air freight is basically charged on weight.
3 *Order processing costs* Small stock levels in the overseas markets, short order processing time and short lead times will tend to result in smaller and more frequent orders from the overseas markets. This will increase the cost of issuing and processing orders.
4 *Cost of holding stock* This cost will vary from one country to another depending upon warehousing availability, labour costs, and the effective cost of money invested in the stock. In the foregoing the bulk of these costs, namely the cost of money, falls upon the manufacturer, so that the solution can be more easily seen. If, however, the overseas agent is financing stock, it will not be so easy to identify the potential savings of a reduced lead time which would involve changes in the distributor's margins etc.
5 *Production costs* The effect of these changes on production scheduling and economics would have to be carefully examined. For example, if the products were marketed in local-language packs, it might be necessary not to label any pack until after receipt of order.
6 *Existing air shipments* Most shippers who distribute by sea also use air for emergency shipments. If these emergency shipments are of significant proportions and involve high air rates due to the size of shipments coming under the lower weight break points, a saving results from a total use of air at high-weight break points. For example, a shipper may on average send 5000 kilos of emergency air consignment a year, at an average rate of fifty pence a kilo, because each shipment is relatively small. But distribution by air might result in the effective cost of this 5000 kilos being only twenty pence a kilo—a saving of 5000 × 30p = £1500 because they would form part of larger shipments at a lower rate.

Custom-built Products

Custom-built products cannot be stocked and at first sight it might appear that no distribution problem is involved except in respect of transporting them in good condition to the customer. The method of packing may have some relevance to the condition in which the products arrive and the speed of transportation may have some bearing on the satisfaction of the customer.

But, as the following example shows, a careful examination of the whole process, including manufacture in one country and sale in another, can often produce some rewarding conclusions.

This example concerns a British firm which exports a custom-built machine to the USA where the length of delivery time affects the volume of sales. Sales are made through a distributor in the USA who buys from the British exporter and then re-sells to his own customers. The machines are supplied exactly as the distributor receives them.

For some time sales have been steadily dropping and the distributor is well aware that the reason for this is the emergence of local competitors who are able to offer shorter delivery dates at almost the same price and quality level. The only way he can compete on delivery is by air freighting the machines. So he is faced with three basic questions:

1 Will sales increase if the delivery time is reduced?
2 How much profit will be earned from the increase in sales?
3 How much does the reduction in delivery time cost?

The cost comparison is as follows:

	Sea Cost (£)	Air Cost (£)
Manufacturer's FOB price:	100	100
CIF New York price:	125	135
Price to customer:	175	175
Profit:	50	40

The following formula can be used to calculate the minimum percentage increase in the sales that is required to justify the additional cost of air:

$$\frac{\text{GROSS PROFIT}}{\text{Gross Profit less additional cost of air}}$$

$$\frac{50}{40} = 1.25 = 125 - 100 = 25\%$$

The distributor does not believe that improved delivery will increase sales by as much as twenty-five per cent, so it does not pay him to use air freight. He would accept the possibility of a fifteen per cent increase, but not more.

Next, he considers a price increase as a means of paying for the air freight. On the assumption of a fifteen per cent sales increase, the price increase necessary to retain his existing gross profit would be only about £4 per machine but the market is very price-sensitive and he feels it extremely unlikely that he could get the fifteen per cent increase if the price went up.

However, it occurs to him that the exporter will also benefit from an increase in sales so he asks him if he would be prepared to contribute to the cost of air freight by dropping his price a little.

The manufacturer's gross profit is fifteen per cent and he quickly calculates that, to avoid a reduction in total gross profit, he cannot afford to drop the price by more than £2 for a fifteen per cent increase in sales.

This is no good to the distributor because, using the formula given previously, he would still require a nineteen per cent increase in sales to avoid a reduction in his total gross profit, calculated as follows:

$$\frac{50}{42} = 1.19 = 119 - 100 = 19\%$$

There seems to be no way out of the impasse when the manufacturer suddenly remembers that he is operating at below capacity and can therefore increase production by fifteen per cent without any increase in fixed costs. The cost breakdown per unit is:

Fixed costs	£25
Variable costs	£60
Gross Profit	£15

He then figures out the situation on the assumption that price is decreased by £5 to £95 and based on existing sales of 100 machines a year.

Unit price (£)	Sales	Fixed costs (£)	Variable costs (£)	Profit (£)
100	10 000	2500	6000	1500
95	10 925	2500	6900	1525

FIGURE 9:4 MANUFACTURER'S INCREASED SALES PROFIT

Even on a price decrease of £5, he still raises his total gross profit by £25. And now the distributor finds air freight a viable proposition.

Unit FOB price (£)	Sales FOB	Sales CIF	Sales to customer	Profit (£)
100	10 000	12 500	17 500	5000
95	10 925	14 950	20 100	5150

FIGURE 9:5 DISTRIBUTOR'S INCREASED SALES PROFIT

So, by taking all relevant factors into consideration, it is possible not only to arrest the decline in sales but also to increase them.

Most international traders would agree, however, that such a solution is unlikely in practice because communication is rarely that close between an exporter and an overseas selling agent. If the selling organisation is a subsidiary then the right organisation in the parent company may well yield the optimum solution.

But, for the vast body of firms selling through agents, the probable result of the situation described above would be eventual market decline, with the exporter saying how difficult it is to get good agents, and the agent fulminating against an apparent lack of understanding on the part of his principal.

It is insufficiently recognised by exporters that it rarely pays an agent to exploit a market in depth. He earns the greatest income by having as many principals as possible and skimming the cream from all of them. In this way, he achieves the greatest return per unit of selling cost. Unless the exporter is prepared to assume major financial responsibility for the greater element of risk involved in developing a market in depth he will never be able to extract the maximum benefit from it.

10

The effect of organisation on profitability

"The reasonable man adapts himself to the World: The unreasonable one persists in trying to adapt the World to himself. Therefore all progress depends on the unreasonable man"

GEORGE BERNARD SHAW

The effect of organisation on industrial and commercial efficiency is a subject that has been receiving much attention in recent years. A business concern relies on people with natural fears, ambitions and doubts. Each has different skills, different weaknesses. The interrelationship of these skills and weaknesses determines, to a very large extent, the efficiency with which the company functions. When theorists write about organisational structure, they often overlook the fact that the framework of any individual company must necessarily depend on the personalities that it has. A strong man in a particular function may give that function an undue weight in the administration of the company. A weak personality might result in the inability of the function to exercise the influence that it ought to have. One cannot take a theoretical organisation and fit the people one has into it. The people determine the effective organisation, no matter what titles they are given and it is foolish to ignore this fact. Everyone knows firms where the real influence is exerted not by the titular head but by a deputy or some other person in the hierarchy.

Ideal Organisation

Needless to say, a company striving towards optimum efficiency must first of all consider the ideal organisation it needs and then, over a long-term period, it should seek to breed and educate the type of people required to make it work. This involves careful timing and far-sighted judgement, with a clear idea by top management of the goal towards which it is striving and with effective management development policies to see the goal is achieved.

Nowadays, when managements are becoming more conscious of the importance of distribution, and of the amount of money it is costing to distribute their goods, they have sought to give the distribution function more significance within the organisational structure. But, for all the reasons mentioned above, and many more, this can create more problems that it solves. Perhaps the best way to appreciate the difficulty is to consider the structure of a typical medium-sized company which is representative in the sense that it has a significant cost of distribution and a typical management organisation. The company manufactures five different sizes of pumps. The engineering quality of the product is renowned and sales are made in over thirty overseas countries. In addition, there is a very significant sales volume in the UK of over one million pounds a year. The organisation of this company is shown in Figure 10:1 and it gives due emphasis to those functions that conventionally fall into the distribution category—shipping, transport and warehousing.

To understand the type of problems that may exist, it may be rewarding to examine each senior executive as a human being as well as an executive, to see the sort of influences that can grow up in a business.

Management Structure

The key fact about Mr Springer is his age. He is sixty-four years old and shortly due for retirement. He has worked with the company all his life and has made his way up from the shop floor. He is a capable, down-to-earth engineering man who understands the problems of production and who has a shrewd sense of profit and loss. He has worked with his three principal managers, Hepworth, Brown and Fenwick, for a number of years and has complete confidence in them. He is not of an age to think much in terms of innovation and although he likes to feel he keeps up to date, the truth is that he is a little bit suspicious of so-called modern management techniques which, he is firmly convinced, are no substitute for sound shop-floor practice and a clear statement of the cost of production. If he thinks about distribution at all, it is only in the sense that the goods have got to be dispatched to the customer who, one way or another, must pay the costs involved.

Robert Hepworth, the Production Director, is, in many respects, cast in the mould of his superior. An extremely good production man, he is completely on top of his job and there are few more efficiently organised machine shops and assembly shops than his in the country. He genuinely believes that the only really important activity in the company is to obtain maximum utilisation from production machines and men. He recognises that there has to be a selling function but he is inclined to exercise the natural propensity of all production men in believing that the real job of the sales department is to obtain orders of a type, in a quantity, and at a time that permits optimum utilisation of workshops. He feels he does not get sufficient warning from "sales" about the product mix of future orders. They should be prepared to commit themselves to a production programme farther ahead and then ensure that the product is sold.

Distribution, to him, largely means the finished goods warehouse for which he is responsible. He recognises the need to run it at the lowest unit cost and he counts himself lucky to have Bill Jones to look after it for him. Jones is a well-experienced, practical man running his warehouse with clockwork efficiency. It has been firmly impressed upon him that the value of stock in the finished warehouse should not exceed a quarter of a million pounds and, in consultation with his supervisor, he sees that this instruction is carried out. He will not accept, from the assembly shop, any pumps that place him over his limit unless he gets

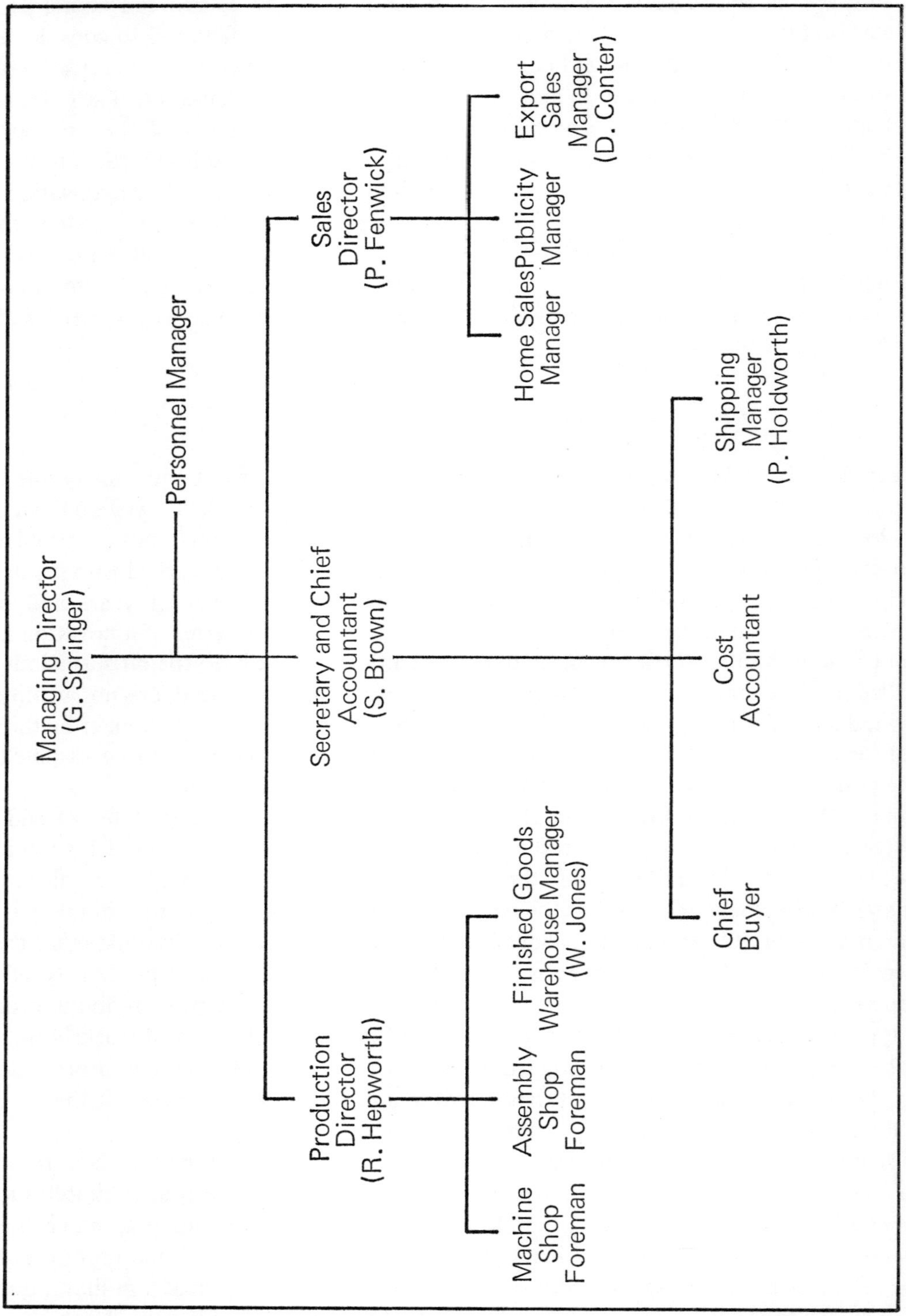

FIGURE 10:1 MANAGEMENT STRUCTURE

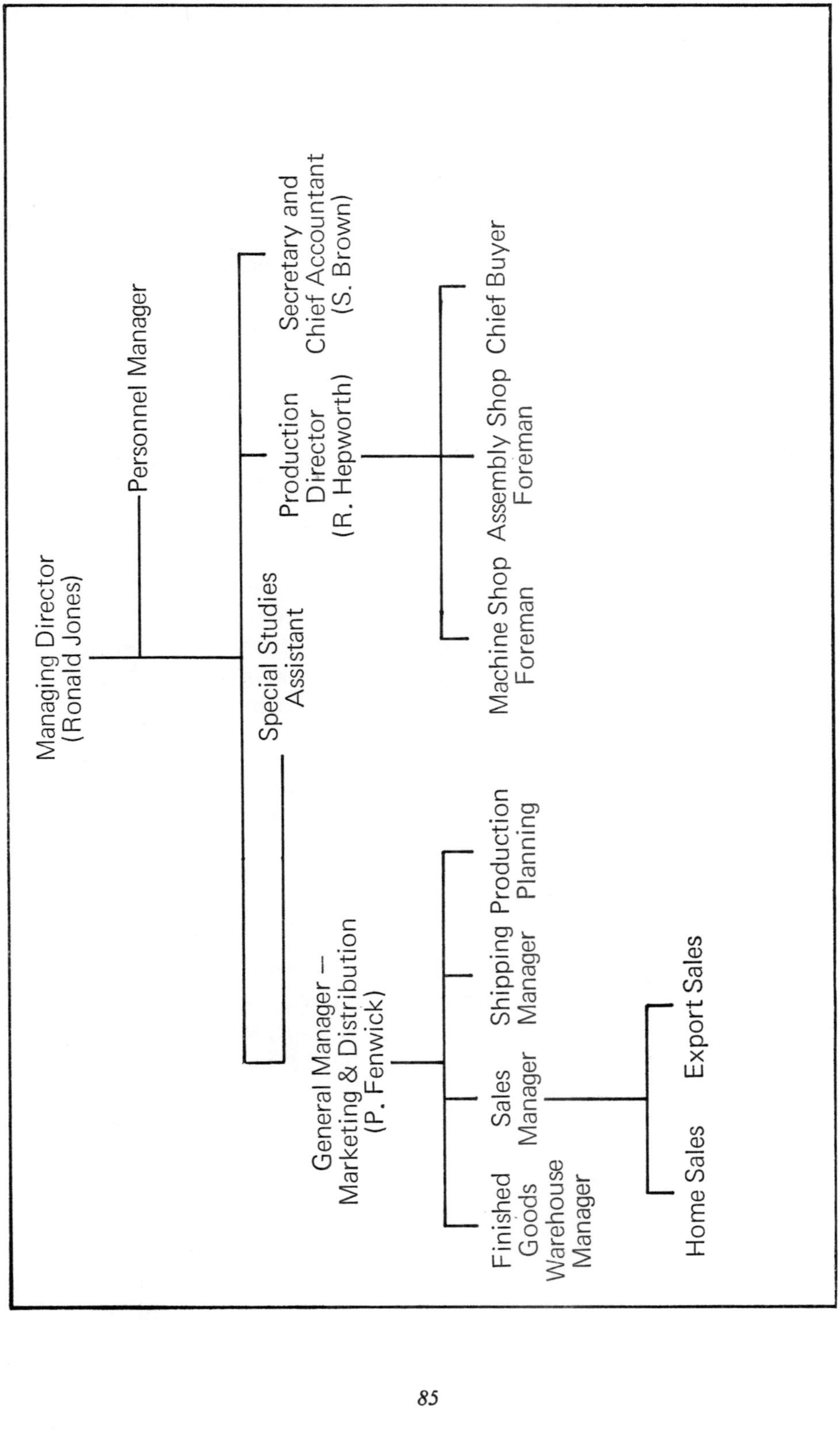

FIGURE 10:2 RE-ORGANISED MANAGEMENT STRUCTURE

specific authority from Mr Hepworth, and no equipment leaves his building unless it is supported by the proper documentation.

Stanley Brown, at fifty-five, is the eldest of the three senior managers reporting to Mr Springer. He has been with the company for thirty years and is still uneasily aware of the fact that he is not a fully qualified accountant. He is a capable man and has served the company well, but inevitably, because of the deep misgivings within him about his security, he has sought throughout his years as secretary and chief accountant to make his position as impregnable as possible. He had many battles with the previous production director before he obtained control of the buying function, and he has had charge of the shipping and transport function ever since that day, twenty years previously, when he gratefully took it over from a sales manager who considered it an unpleasant chore.

Because of the high percentage of export trade, the shipping and transport function has assumed a reasonable significance in the firm, and Mr Holdworth, the Shipping Manager, has now been doing the job for fifteen years. He is familiar with all the rates and methods of shipment and would be very surprised if anyone were to question that his dominant purpose in life was to send pumps from one place to another at the lowest unit cost. He tends to shy away from salesmen from a carrier who might suggest that a higher rate for faster transport, can, perhaps, be offset by savings elsewhere in the distribution system. If any sneaking doubts flicker into his mind from time to time about new developments taking place in distribution techniques, he swiftly supresses them by reassuring himself that his job must be to ship goods as cheaply as possible. Therefore, this must be in the company's best interests. He is not responsible for the packing and warehousing functions, which are looked after by Bill Jones in the production department. His staff are concerned solely with export, transport and shipping documentation.

Finally, Peter Fenwick, the Sales Director. Only thirty-five years old, he is the newest member of the management team, brought in five years ago to replace the then retiring sales director and, during his stay with the firm, he has made a considerable contribution towards the growth of sales. He is paid a bonus geared to the sales he is able to achieve each year and is convinced that it is the *raison d'être* of the company to produce, manufacture and dispatch the pumps he is able to sell. He has some responsibility for profitability because he and the chief accountant jointly fix prices between them. His strongest motivation is towards gettings orders and he measures his success specifically by the extent of the order book. In this he is at one with the Managing Director, Mr Springer, who also judges the sales director purely by the volume of sales. Fenwick has two managers reporting to him, one responsible for home sales and the other for overseas sales. The Export Manager, Don Conter, is only twenty-nine years old and the age disparity tends to set him at a more junior level to the home sales manager, who is forty-five years old and who has been with the company all his working life. Don Conter is more of an overseas representative than a manager; he has never had complete authority over the appointment and dismissal of agents, which Peter Fenwick reserves to himself, partly because he likes the opportunity of overseas travel. His activity is largely confined to visiting agents in order to call upon individual customers with them. He discusses the agent's problems and brings these back to Peter Fenwick, but he does not have the experience, nor indeed the incentive, to look beyond the simple function of assisting the agent to obtain specific orders. Inevitably, advocacy on behalf of export sales is weaker in the sales department's policy making.

This is a picture of a not untypical British company, medium sized, well established and reasonably successful. If the pen sketches of each executive seem, by implication, to be critical, it must be remembered that the manner in which this management are behaving is entirely normal.

When, as a management team, they confer together with the managing director, each departmental manager is going to be thinking in terms of his own success, his own rewards and his own prospects. He is going to want to see external recognition of the manner in which he does his job and he will seek to get this measured in a way that reflects most favourably upon him. It is only in management books that executives are entirely objective.

In such a setting, the only man who can balance the varying claims and aspirations of each department is the managing director, and he will tend to do this on the basis of his own experience and prejudice and, of course, on the basis of the information available to him. Mr Springer has access to conventional information on the cost of production and selling and on the general level of overheads, and he is satisfied that this is sufficient for him to control profitability. The accounting system does not—nor has he ever reasoned that it should do—seek to analyse the various overhead cost areas in any detail.

Before very long, the day comes for Mr Springer to retire, and he is replaced by a forty-one-year-old accountant who is brought in from outside the company. Mr Ronald Jones is a man of weighty industrial and commercial background but with no formal technical qualifications. He spends his first few weeks talking with the various managers in both senior and middle ranks, studies the data available to him and spends a good deal of time at home thinking about the basic policy he ought to pursue against a background of growing international competition in the pump manufacturing industry. Quite clearly, each manager is competent and well equipped to do each job. But the more he studies the situation the more he comes to the conclusion that the organisational structure, does, or could, have a restricting effect upon the total economic prosperity of the company. For example, he asked himself a number of questions and, within the existing organisation, he could not find the answers to:

1 Could gross profit be increased by restricting the volume of sales and altering the product mix?
2 Can sales be increased by raising the level of stock in the finished warehouse to a point that would avoid stock-outs?
3 Could overseas sales be increased if the goods were delivered more quickly?
4 Is it more economic to have the workshops function at less than optimum utilisation?

Analysis of Trade-off Economics

It was clear that the answers to these questions were only going to emerge if someone with the right type of inquiring and analytical mind were overseeing all related functions. So he decided to change the organisation to that shown in Figure 10:2. What he wanted was one man co-ordinating sales, storage, transport and, perhaps rather unexpectedly, production planning, because he could see that there was some sort of relationship between the volume and cost of production, the volume and cost of storage, the types of transport and the sales mix and he wanted to quantify that relationship. He decided that Peter Fenwick was the man who was most likely to have the mental flexibility to cope with this task so he put him in charge of a newly formed department. He gave a lot of thought to what he should call him. He could, quite logically, perhaps, describe him as marketing director except this might inflame the natural prejudice of technical people against sales. He even toyed with the idea of using the American title of "physical distribution management director" but he felt that the use of the word "physical" might give rise to misunderstandings.

The trouble with using "distribution director" was that he believed that distribution to most people in the firm meant transport and warehousing—not very senior functions—and he did not want to use a title that might tend to lessen the importance he wanted to see attached to the position. He could not think of an ideal solution and in the end he decided on "general manager—marketing and distribution" as best representing the type of philosophy he was trying to promote.

He had a number of difficulties to cope with from his other two senior managers. Robert Hepworth was, quite frankly, appalled that anybody connected with sales should have anything to do with production planning; it required a lot of reasoned explanation and reassurance that there would be no interference in the actual administration of his department before he reluctantly agreed to the experiment. The function of production planning was to determine what should be produced and the quantity—not to interfere in how it was produced. It seemed logical on the other hand that production should take over responsibility for the buying function and this was done.

Stanley Brown's deep misgivings about his personal position were allayed by giving him a five-year contract which compensated him for the loss of the buying and the shipping functions.

Production Planning

The production planning function was conceived by Ronald Jones and requires a little further explanation. As has already been mentioned, five different categories of pumps are produced by the factory. One of the major problems that the company faced was that the economics of production differed for each type of pump to some extent and that the sales mix varied from one territory to another, thus making the forecasting of the mix difficult. Study in this direction was started by endeavouring to improve the accuracy of the sales forecast, both at home and overseas, and by seeking to attach to it reasonable estimates of the errors inherent in the forecast. The production planning people were then asked to draw up a schedule of the economics of various batch quantities. The point that had to be established was:

> Could it, in certain circumstances, be cheaper to produce in less than so-called economic batch quantities when this increased cost was measured against the saving of finished goods inventory and work-in-progress?

The warehouse manager was told to forget about the one quarter million pounds limit of stock and to start computing how much stock was needed for various levels of in-stock reliability.

The shipping manager was requested to investigate all the various transport alternatives that existed to all countries of sale, and to compare the direct costs involved in each method, applicable to packing, documentation, insurance and so on, and then to draw up a schedule of all the lead times involved.

The export manager was asked to contact all overseas agents and find out the sales lost due to non-availability of particular types of pumps, within a specified order period, and if an increase of sales could be realistically expected if this availability were improved.

As all these various investigations got under way, Peter Fenwick started to receive complaints from his managers about the amount of time these studies were taking them and since he felt that the analysis and interpretation of the results required independent and expert appraisal, he decided to appoint a special studies assistant, not only to help in the compilation of data but also, to evaluate them for him.

Ronald Jones knew that, in order to form a true economic picture, all the variables in the equation had to be taken into account. It is no good slavishly manufacturing in theoretical economic batches if this results in too much stock of slow-moving items. It is silly to wait for orders before manufacturing if this results in lost sales of items that can be readily forecast. There is no sense in keeping to a theoretical stock level if a higher stock level would result in increased sales yielding an incremental profit higher than the incremental stock cost. If a faster mode of transport is going to help an overseas agent to increase his sales profitably, then it is negligent not to pay the higher rate. The only way to find out the optimum solution is to collect all relevant information and analyse it intelligently.

Ensuing Advantages

After a year, some of the advantages of this new activity began to emerge. In some areas of activity, this meant that certain operations were carried out at more than the lowest unit cost. But overall profitability increased because the company now knew that an apparent economic disadvantage in one area was more than offset by an economic advantage in another area. This meant that the attitudes of the individual managers changed. They had to start thinking more as a team than as individuals. It became important for Peter Fenwick to impress upon them that their success was going to be judged more by their contribution towards the team objective rather than by an individual performance in a particular function.

After a year, Robert Hepworth grudgingly conceded that the new organisation was yielding benefits to him. He was now getting a fixed production schedule from the new production planning section sufficiently far ahead to enable him to plan and operate with the minimum of disruption. The overall profit had increased and each manager was contributing his part to the increase. It will be noted that all this was done without changing any of the managers. The talents of the individual managers were put to better use and dovetailed more effectively into a common objective. It could not have been achieved without the change in organisation introduced by Ronald Jones.

It must not, of course, be assumed that the examples of organisation shown in this chapter are relevant to all companies. Industries vary widely and their organisational needs are correspondingly different. What can be urged, with some emphasis, is that any organisation, if it is to be effective in a distribution context, must have someone in authority, even the chief executive if necessary, responsible for exploiting all the opportunities that may exist for trade-off economies.

Appendix

Stock models that show the effect of reduced lead times on average inventory levels

---

Assumptions

The following assumptions are made:

1 *Demand* The same assumed frequency distribution of demand is used for all three models. The actual sequence of demand over the fifty-week period was determined by random selection. The amount of each weekly demand is arbitrarily divided into two parts so that a re-order can be shown precisely when the re-order point is reached in models 1 and 2. In model 3, because of the introduction of air consignments, there are four occasions (27th, 31st, 34th and 48th weeks) when re-orders are made before the re-order point is reached; this has the effect of making the average stock balance over the year very slightly higher than it need be in comparison with models 1 and 2. To avoid this would have necessitated a further subdivision of demand in model 3 and this would have over-complicated the illustration.

2 *EOQ* In calculating the economic order quantity (EOQ) it is assumed that:

1 Annual demand (R) is 5200 units, averaging 100 units per week
2 Weight of unit is one lb
3 Value of unit taken into stock (C) is £1
4 Possession cost (I) is 25% of stock investment
5 Acquisition cost (A) is £3

The economic order quantity (EOQ) therefore is:

$$\sqrt{\frac{2AR}{IC}} = \sqrt{\frac{2 \times 3 \times 5200}{0.25}} = 353, \text{ say } 350$$

3 *Starting stock balance* This is calculated from (lead time × average weekly usage) + 1 (EOQ) + safety stock.

4 *Re-order point* Except in model 3, this is calculated by:

(lead time × average weekly usage) + safety stock

5 *Lead times* The lead times for the models are:

Model 1—6 weeks
Model 2—3 weeks
Model 3—6 weeks (sea)
7 days (air)

6 *Safety stock* Levels have been set at the minimum necessary to avoid an out-of-stock position:

Model 1—100 units
Model 2— 50 units
Model 3— 10 units

7 *Models* 1, 2 *and* 3 In models 1 and 2, the re-order points are 700 and 350 respectively. In model 3, the cheapest form of transport—involving a lead time of six weeks—is used to cater for average demand. The re-order point for a sea shipment is therefore 600 (6 times weekly average demand), but excluding safety stock. Air transport, involving a lead time of seven days, is used for above-average demand. The re-order rule is first to set a safety stock level, which in model 3 must be at least ten to avoid a run-out. The stock balance is reviewed two weeks before the next sea shipment will arrive. If this balance is less than 210, or twice the average weekly demand plus safety stock, an order is made for air consignment of the short-fall. If the lead time was two weeks, the review would have to be carried out three weeks before the next sea shipment arrived.

The objective in using air transport to reduce stock levels is to have available the shortest possible lead time to cater for variations in demand above the average. A comparison of models 2 and 3 shows that, by airfreighting only 130 units from a total of 4680 (2.8 %) in a year when the air lead time is reduced to seven days, almost as large a reduction in average stock balance is achieved as a total conversion to air would achieve if the air lead time were three weeks. However, the amount on order falls proportionately to a reduction in lead time and this in many instances represents cost savings.

Stock Models That Show the Effect of Reduced Lead Times on Average Inventory Levels

STOCK MODEL 1

WEEK	ISSUES	RECEIPTS	BALANCE	ON ORDER	RE-ORDER QUANTITY
			1 050		
1	50		1 000		
	50		950		
2	40		910		
	40		870		
3	40		830		
	50		780		
4	80		700		350
	30		670	350	
5	60		610	350	
	60		550	350	
6	40		510	350	
	50		460	350	
7	40		420	350	
	40		380	350	
8	30		350	350	350
	60		290	700	
9	40		250	700	
	50		200	700	
10	30	350	520	700	
	40		480	350	
11	50		430	350	
	50		380	350	
12	30		350	350	350
	60		290	700	
13	40		250	700	
	40		210	700	
14	50	350	510	700	
	50		460	350	
15	50		410	350	
	50		360	350	
16	10		350	350	350
	70		280	700	
17	40		240	700	
	50		190	700	
18	40	350	500	700	
	40		460	350	
19	50		410	350	
	50		360	350	
20	10		350	350	350
	80		270	700	
21	40		230	700	
	50		180	700	
22	50	350	480	700	
	60		420	350	
23	70		350	350	350
	40		310	700	
24	40		270	700	
	50		220	700	
25	40		180	700	
	50		130	700	
26	50	350	430	700	
	50		380	350	
27	30		350	350	350
	80		270	700	
28	40		230	700	
	40		190	700	

Stock Models That Show the Effect of Reduced Lead Times on Average Inventory Levels

Stock Model 1 (*continued*)

WEEK	ISSUES	RECEIPTS	BALANCE	ON ORDER	RE-ORDER QUANTITY
29	40	350	500	700	
	50		450	350	
30	40		410	350	
	50		360	350	
31	10		350	350	350
	90		260	700	
32	70		190	700	
	80		110	700	
33	50	350	410	700	
	50		360	350	
34	10		350	350	350
	90		260	700	
35	50		210	700	
	50		160	700	
36	60		100	700	
	60		40	700	
37	40	350	350	700	350
	50		300	700	
38	50		250	700	
	40		210	700	
39	50		160	700	
	60		100	700	
40	50	350	400	700	
	40		360	350	
41	10		350	350	350
	100		250	700	
42	50		200	700	
	50		150	700	
43	50	350	450	700	
	50		400	350	
44	50		350	350	350
	70		280	700	
45	40		240	700	
	60		180	700	
45	50		130	700	
	30		100	700	
47	100	350	350	700	350
	30		320	700	
48	40		280	700	
	40		240	700	
49	60		180	700	
	70		110	700	
50	40	350	420	700	
	40		380	350	
			35 420	52 850	
AVERAGE			354 +	528	= 882

Lead time	6 weeks:	Re-order point	700 units:
EOQ	350 units:	Initial stock balance	1050 units:
Safety stock	100 units:		

Stock Models That Show the Effect of Reduced Lead Times on Average Inventory Levels

STOCK MODEL 2

WEEK	ISSUES	RECEIPTS	BALANCE	ON ORDER	RE-ORDER QUANTITY
			700		
1	50		650		
	50		600		
2	40		560		
	40		520		
3	40		480		
	50		430		
4	80		350		350
	30		320	350	
5	60		260	350	
	60		200	350	
6	40		160	350	
	50		110	350	
7	40	350	420	350	
	40		380		
8	30		350		350
	60		290	350	
9	40		250	350	
	50		200	350	
10	30		170	350	
	40		130	350	
11	50	350	430	350	
	50		380		
12	30		350		350
	60		290	350	
13	40		250	350	
	40		210	350	
14	50		160	350	
	50		110	350	
15	50	350	410	350	
	50		360		
16	10		350		350
	70		280	350	
17	40		240	350	
	50		190	350	
18	40		150	350	
	40		110	350	
19	50	350	410	350	
	50		360		
20	10		350		350
	80		270	350	
21	40		230	350	
	50		180	350	
22	50		130	350	
	60		70	350	
23	70	350	350	350	350
	40		310	350	
24	40		270	350	
	50		220	350	
25	40		180	350	
	50		130	350	
26	50	350	430	350	
	50		380		
27	30		350		350
	80		270	350	
28	40		230	350	
	40		190	350	

Stock Models That Show the Effect of Reduced Lead Times on Average Inventory Levels

Stock Model 2 (*continued*)

WEEK	ISSUES	RECEIPTS	BALANCE	ON ORDER	RE-ORDER QUANTITY
29	40		150	350	
	50		100	350	
30	40	350	410	350	
	50		360		350
31	10		350		
	90		260	350	
32	70		190	350	
	80		110	350	
33	50		60	350	
	50		10	350	
34	10	350	350	350	350
	90		260	350	
35	50		210	350	
	50		160	350	
36	60		100	350	
	60		40	350	
37	40	350	350	350	350
	50		300	350	
38	50		250	350	
	40		210	350	
39	50		160	350	
	60		100	350	
40	50	350	400	350	
	40		360		
41	10		350		350
	100		250	350	
42	50		200	350	
	50		150	350	
43	50		100	350	
	50		50	350	
44	50	350	350	350	350
	70		280	350	
45	40		240	350	
	60		180	350	
46	50		130	350	
	30		100	350	
47	100	350	350	350	350
	30		320	350	
48	40		280	350	
	40		240	350	
49	60		180	350	
	70		110	350	
50	40	350	420	350	
	40		380		
			26 320	27 300	
AVERAGE			263 +	273 =	536

Lead time	3 weeks	Re-order point	350 units
EOQ	350 units	Initial stock balance	700 units
Safety stock	50 units		

Stock Models That Show the Effect of Reduced Lead Times on Average Inventory Levels

STOCK MODEL 3

WEEK	ISSUES	RECEIPTS	BALANCE	ON ORDER	RE-ORDER QUANTITY
			950		
1	50		900		
	50		850		
2	40		810		
	40		770		
3	40		730		
	50		680		
4	80		600		350
	30		570	350	
5	60		510	350	
	60		450	350	
6	40		410	350	
	50		360	350	
7	40		320	350	
	40		280	350	
8	30		250	350	350
	60		190	700	
9	40		150	700	
	50		100	700	
10	30	350	420	700	
	40		380	350	
11	50		330	350	
	50		280	350	
12	30		250	350	350
	60		190	700	
13	40		150	700	
	40		110	700	
14	50	350	410	700	
	50		360	350	
15	50		310	350	
	50		260	350	
16	10		250	350	350
	70		180	700	
17	40		140	700	
	50		90	700	
18	40	350	400	700	
	40		360	350	
19	50		310	350	
	50		260	350	
20	10		250	350	350
	80		170	700	
21	40		130	700	
	50		80	700	
22	50	350	380	700	
	60		320	350	
23	70		250	350	350
	40		210	700	
24	40		170	700	*40
	50		120	740	
25	40	*40	120	740	
	50		70	700	
26	50	350	370	700	
	50		320	350	
27	30		290	350	350
	80		210	700	
28	40		170	700	
	40		130	700	

Stock Models That Show the Effect of Reduced Lead Times an Average Inventory Levels

Stock Model 3 (*continued*)

WEEK	ISSUES	RECEIPTS	BALANCE	ON ORDER	RE-ORDER QUANTITY
29	40	350	440	700	
	50		390	350	
30	40		350	350	
	50		300	350	
31	10		290	350	350
	90		200	700	
32	70		130	700	
	80		50	700	
33	50	350	350	700	
	50		300	350	
34	10		290	350	350
	90		200	700	
35	50		150	700	*60
	50		100	760	
36	60	*60	100	760	
	60		40	700	
37	40	350	350	700	
	50		300	350	
38	50		250	350	350
	40		210	700	
39	50		160	700	
	60		100	700	
40	50	350	400	700	
	40		360	350	
41	10		350	350	
	100		250	350	350
42	50		200	700	*10
	50		150	710	
43	50	*10	110	710	
	50		60	700	
44	50	350	360	700	
	70		290	350	
45	40		250	350	350
	60		190	700	*20
46	50		140	720	
	30	*20	130	720	
47	100		30	700	
	30	350	350	700	
48	40		310	350	
	40		270	350	350
49	60		210	700	
	70		140	700	
50	40		100	700	
	40		60	700	
			27 890	51 710	
AVERAGE			279 +	517 =	796

* Air shipments

Sea lead time	6 weeks	Re-order point	600 units
Air lead time	7 days	Initial stock balance	950 units
Safety stock	10 units		

Index